3

Game & the English Landscape

Two Gentlemen Going Shooting, or 'Shooting II' – one of a set of four paintings of the Midland countryside for Mr J. Bradford in 1770. George Stubbs.

GAME
& the
ENGLISH
LANDSCAPE

The Influence of the Chase
on Sporting Art and Scenery

Anthony Vandervell
&
Charles Coles

Foreword by the Duke of Wellington

DEBRETT'S PEERAGE LIMITED
MCMLXXX

Published by Debrett's Peerage Limited,
73–77 Britannia Road London SW6

First published 1980

ISBN 0905649 32 X

Produced by Edition, 25 Lloyd Baker Street, London WC1

Designed by Tom Carter

Setting by Input Typesetting Ltd., London SW19
Printed by de Lange/van Leer b.v., Deventer, Holland

Printed in Holland.

Two thirds of the authors' royalties from this work will be contributed to The Game Conservancy of Great Britain.

Note on the Illustrations

A wide variety of sporting paintings and prints has been selected to enhance and illustrate the text. The choice has not been easy: there is little point in using pictures of horses or hounds in which a landscape has been contrived. Many paintings are still in private hands. Some will not have been used as illustrations before as they may have hung on the walls of country houses since they were painted; others are not in collections which are on public view. Although sporting scenes of horses and hunting predominated, a large number of game shooting and many rural fishing pictures were painted – some of which have been selected to illustrate our theme of the landscape around us. Often by lesser-known artists they are nevertheless an integral part of our sporting inheritance.

Contents

	Foreword	7
	Authors' Preface	9
CHAPTER I	The Hunter's Imprint on the Landscape	11
CHAPTER II	The Beginnings of the Hunting Sports	21

When cave man hunted and drew pictures – Deer hunting in a wild landscape – Falconry or Hawking: the sport of hunting in the sky – The close of the 16th century and change – Early fox-hunting – Horse breeding and racing – Coursing – Fowling and shooting – Game reserves become sporting demesnes – The origins and history of the pheasant

| CHAPTER III | The Evolution of Farming and Forestry | 47 |

The Age of timber – Climate and soil – The old farming practices – The enclosures – The influence of changes in farming – Landed estates and the country house – Sporting landowners and their estates – More recent trends

| CHAPTER IV | Sporting Art as a Pictorial Archive | 59 |
| CHAPTER V | Rural Sports and the Landscape | 77 |

Speed: the factor in the Chase from the 18th century – Shooting flying: the supreme challenge – Racing gets well established – The hare: a link between the stag and modern fox-hunting – The fox: the quest for speed in sport – The partridge: the bird that created shooting flying – French partridges are introduced – The later developments to guns – The pheasant and driven shooting in the Victorian century – Walking-up and driving pheasants – Woodlands come in for much attention – The Big Shots – The red grouse

| CHAPTER VI | Sporting Waters | 117 |

Wildfowlers and the landscape – Anglers and their environment

| CHAPTER VII | Designs for Game | 131 |

Planning for game: some aesthetic considerations – New features in the landscape: gravel pits and reservoirs – Managing wildlife and game

CHAPTER VIII	Pressures on the Countryside	147
	Bibliography	153
	Acknowledgements	155
	Illustration Sources	156
	Index	157

Foreword

by

His Grace the Duke of Wellington, MVO, OBE, MC, DL
President of The Game Conservancy of Great Britain

Unpalatable as it may be to those who disapprove of field sports, few would deny that we in this country owe a great debt of gratitude to those who, down through the centuries, have inspired and upheld our great heritage of sporting art. British sporting painters stand supreme in their particular field. The artistic world would be a poorer place without Stubbs, Herring, Munnings and many others.

What must never be forgotten, however, is that none of these artists would have flourished without the sustained patronage of sportsmen, who, as either landowners or just followers of the Chase, indulged their passion for field sports, not only in the field but by their encouragement of artists and writers.

Less obvious, but no less important, is the part played by these same men in the creation of the diminishing rural landscape which we continue to enjoy in these islands. How dull it would be, without the forests and coverts, the hedgerows and stone walls, and the great parks created by these men to shelter stock and game, and to harbour the fox and the deer. How uninteresting, too, would be our rivers – whether turbulent or placid – if generations of fishermen had not ensured their continued well-being and purity, and the preservation of their banks in their natural state.

Compare the great, featureless agricultural plains of the Continent – ecological deserts – as inhospitable to game as they are to wildlife; and our limpid streams so unlike many of the continental rivers which rush their turgid waters to the sea, regimented and constrained by straightjackets of concrete and earth.

In this well-researched book the authors have drawn together these two important threads of our tradition and our culture to present a picture which at last pays tribute to sportsmen of the past who have contributed so much to what is called, these days, the quality of life. It is something which was long overdue, and the authors are to be warmly commended for their initiative.

Wellington

7

305 The LADIES SHOOTING PONEY.

From the Original Picture by John Collet in the Possession of Carington Bowles.

8

Authors' Preface

Our intention in writing this book was to show how so many of the traditional rural sports have made a significant contribution to the shape, texture and general attractiveness of our countryside which would not have come about if food and timber production alone had been the concern of the land-user. In many places, the aesthetic effect created by earlier generations of hunters – using the term in its broadest sense – has been long lasting. Today, in a shrinking countryside, the continuing synthesis between shotgun and covert, rod and riverbank is of increasing relevance.

To illustrate our ideas, we looked at many of the great collections of British sporting art and landscape paintings both at home and abroad, including those of Her Majesty the Queen, and the Mellon Collection at Yale in the United States. We visited many galleries, private houses, print shops and libraries, and consulted experts in various fields, and it soon became apparent that we could not ignore a second theme. These rural sports had shaped not only our woodlands, farms, hedgerows and wetlands, but had also influenced an individual school of British artists – a group quite distinct from the painters of landscapes – the sporting artists, who began with Richard Barlow and reached a high point with George Stubbs.

Had there been no fox-hunting or shooting, Alken might have painted poultry, cricket matches, or cattle in the meadows; and Pollard, Wolstenholme and Sartorius might have achieved fame by portraying archery, sheep-shearing and village bowling-greens. Clearly, our sporting art owes something to the shotgun, the foxhound and the fishing-rod, as well as to the many generations of sportsmen who became fascinated by the game animals and other quarry species which have so often been its inspiration.

The imprint of the hunter on the rural landscape has probably been more marked in England than in any other country in the world. Certainly it is a subject which has been far from fully appreciated: sometimes blatantly misunderstood, and at times not understood at all. We hope that by interpreting the works of sporting landscape artists and social historians in their role as archivists and biographers, we can trace some of the many subtle changes which have taken place in the countryside around us. Perhaps we may also be able to judge how much of the change was directly affected by man because he was sympathetic to conserving the habitat of the wild creatures he hunted.

Summer 1980

Anthony Vandervell
Charles Coles

The Game Conservancy,
Fordingbridge,
Hampshire,
England

The Sussex Weald seen from Duncton
Hill.

I
The Hunter's Imprint on the Landscape

The sporting landscape today is a fascinating and vital part of social history and our national heritage, since most of the countryside we now see around us was moulded by our ancestors. Probably more of the trees growing today were planted by our forebears than grew by natural regeneration, and some of the finest examples are found in the preserves of many old deer parks. Much of our landscape has been largely contrived by man as a direct outcome of his interest in hunting, the husbandry of animals and their habitat, with results unique to the British Isles. The effects visible today are often such as were described in Victorian times as garden landscaping on the grand scale. How much is perhaps attributable to Lancelot 'Capability' Brown or Humphrey Repton and how much to chance is difficult to discern.

However, the scenery with which we are concerned is not represented by extremes of grandeur – vast forests, wild mountains or geological masterpieces – but by the intimate mosaic of fields and woods, such as one sees

Haldon Hall near Exeter, in the summer of 1780. An example of countryside with immense sporting possibilities. Francis Towne.

11

on many English estates. This countryside embraces farms and scattered hamlets, old parklands and hedgebanks, vistas and tracks; rounded chalk downs and alluvial valleys, skyscape and landscape; greens and browns, and blues and greys. All these aspects combine to make a picturesque and interesting whole: apparently haphazard, yet organised. As Professor W. G. Hoskins said: 'The English landscape itself – to those who know how to read it aright, is the richest historical record we possess.'

By the second half of the eighteenth century, with most rural sports well established and enclosures in some areas nearing completion, the sporting island scenery was ready to be painted in its many differing guises by a long list of artists, whose work has continued to record the changing countryside up to the present day.

Extensive areas of the countryside today owe their present form as much to our long sporting history in its widest sense, as to the evolution of agriculture, forestry and social development over the centuries, and, in particular, that of the last three hundred years or so. This spirit of the

Two deer parks – Badminton in Gloucestershire (*below*) and Melton Constable in Norfolk, from prints by Kip *c*1710. They show the large areas given over to fallow and red deer. In Badminton a deer paddock course can be seen; Silk Wood is in the bottom left corner.

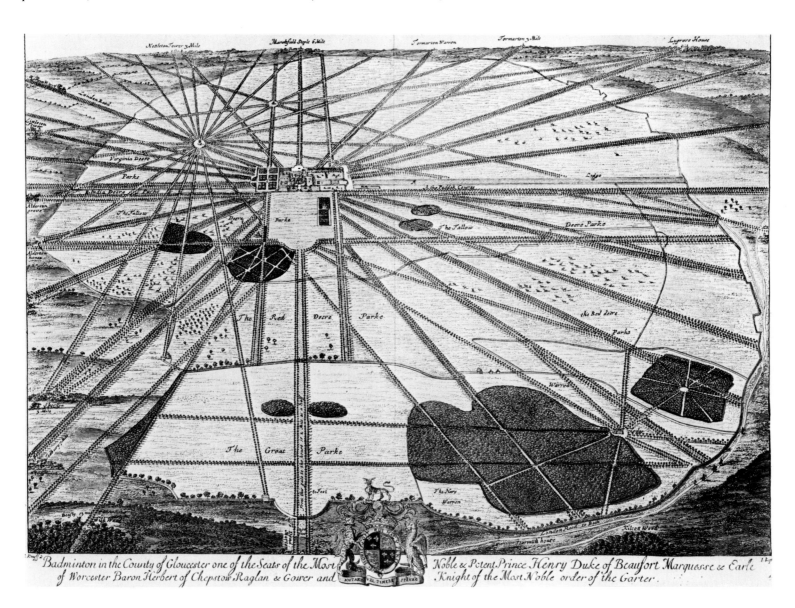

Badminton in the County of Gloucester one of the Seats of the Most Noble & Potent Prince Henry Duke of Beaufort Marquesse & Earle of Worcester Baron Herbert of Chepstow Raglan & Gower and Knight of the Most Noble order of the Garter.

Chase in the mediaeval forest was kindled under the Norman kings, and impressed itself on the history of the countryside. Forests, then woodlands and parks, were laid out and fenced – and often reshaped or planted – to enhance their sporting and amenity characteristics. For instance, one of the early Great Parks in England was formed about 1124 at the manor of Woodstock in Oxfordshire, and later became the grounds of Blenheim Palace.

The concept of a park, as a place for enclosing deer, hares and other game animals, both for sport and food, as if it were a store house, is admirably described in *The Sportsman's Dictionary*, originally published in 1735 (3rd edition, 1785). The spelling in the following extract has been modernised:

'A Park should have three sorts of land in it, viz. mountainous and barren, hilly and yet fertile, plain and fruitful. The mountainous part thereof should be well covered with high woods, at least a third part thereof; the downs

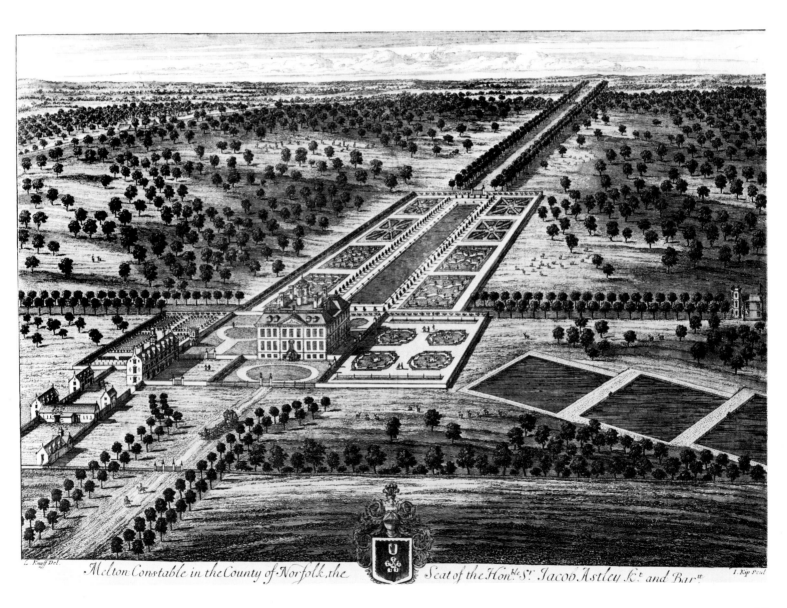

Melton Constable in the County of Norfolk, the Seat of the Hon.ble S.r Jacob Astley K.t and Bar.tt

and hills, should have one third part coppices and low woods; and the plains at least one third part meadows with some arable for corn.

'A Park should not want a river to run through some part of it; also it ought to have a small brook or spring, but if Nature denies these conveniences, you must supply it by ponds, made to receive and preserve rains that fall; and such ponds will be very profitable for fish and fowl, in some of which may be made a decoy.

'You should have your Park well stored with many trees, as oak, beech and chestnut, which are not difficult to be had, and are quick of growth, especially the two last, and they exceed the former also in sweetness and goodness; neither should apple, pear and plum trees be wanting; all affording good food for them.

'You should also have your Park well enclosed, if possible with a brick or stone wall: or for want of that with a pale of sound oak, so high and

Map of Middlesex and Hertfordshire by Jansson, *c*1650. The green spots on the landscape indicate the many imparked estates preserved for deer.

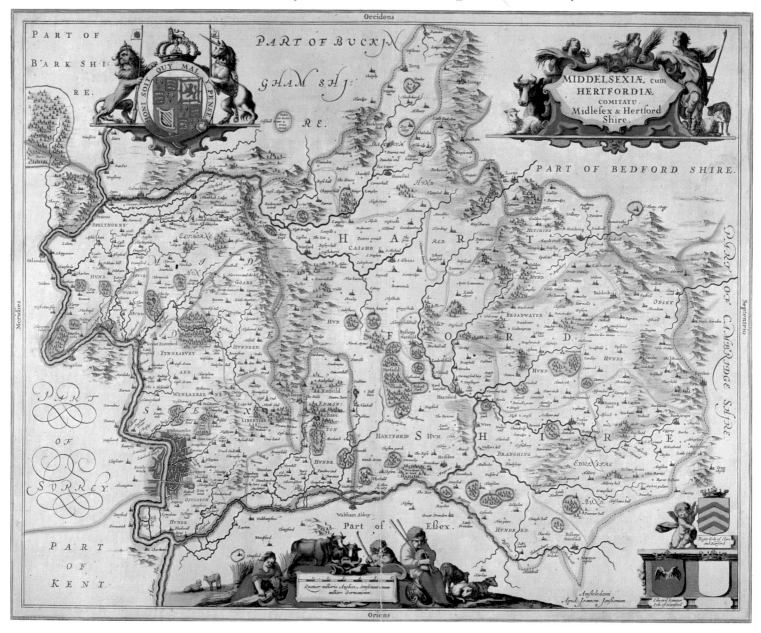

close joined, that neither badger nor cat can creep through, nor wolf nor fox can leap over. . .

'Some part of the high wood may afford a heronry, and some part of the middle may be for a rabbit or hare warren. In the whole, you may breed young colts and horses. . .

'There should be at least five or six enclosures in your park, that you may shut out, and let in, your deer, as you see occasion; sometimes all together in your high woods, where in cold frosts and snow they may be sheltered and fed by the keepers with hay and provender.'

Certainly many parks and hayes – less formal enclosures for deer – were carved out in much earlier times, not solely for hunting, but as reserves for food. Kenneth Whitehead in *Deer and Their Management* mentions that there were some thirty-one parks and more than seventy hayes by the end of the eleventh century.

Examples still survive of the many deer parks carved out of the countryside for personal hunting – from which all but the privileged hunters and the deer were excluded – though most are now only recognisable by their fine old oaks and other forests trees and their designation 'Park', and sometimes 'Chase', which often appears on old maps. In Saxton's maps of 1575–80, over seven hundred deer parks throughout the land were shown, though by that time they were maintained for pleasure and not, as originally, for the food they supplied. So great was the interest in hunting in England that there were probably more parks here than in the whole of Europe. In 1614 Francis Bacon wrote: 'Forests, parks, chases, they are a noble portion of the King's prerogative; they are the verdure of the King, they are the first marks of honour and nobility, and the ornament of a flourishing Kingdom. . .' ('Verdure' – vert or green hue – included virtually every plant growing within a forest, bearing green leaf which may hide or cover a deer. Verderers were judicial officers of the King's forest whose main duty was to watch over the wild game and the green growth.)

Later large areas of woodland coverts were planted mainly for hard timber and pheasant shooting. Lawrence Rawstorne had much to say in *Gamonia, or the Art of Preserving Game* (1837) about tree planting and woodlands, as related to pheasant management, and he shows how contemporary pheasant management was not only instrumental in clothing bare hillsides with trees – thus changing the skyline – but was also responsible for many other permanent alterations in the countryside. He wrote:

'Nothing adds so much to the beauty of a country as to be well covered with wood. Fine straight-growing trees are of themselves beautiful objects. They set off to greater advantage a varied surface, they can make even a dead flat appear pleasing and attractive. But it is not only in a picturesque point of view that they are of use; it is also an agricultural one.

'The warmth and shelter they afford are such that an almost new climate is created by them. Vegetation is assisted and forwarded. Cattle seek to repose under their branches; all farming stock thrive so much the better for their fostering aid. . .

'The respective position of the coverts being arranged, great attention is to be paid to the ground on which they are to be made. In the choice of this, there is no better guide than to fix on that which is already much

An aerial view of part of Sussex, showing the irregular shapes of fields formed from clearings in the old forest, with a few later hedgerows.

Landscape above Henley showing the Thames and the regular hedges of enclosure in the background. In the foreground is the Prince of Wales with grooms and falconers in royal livery. John Wootton; dated 1742. Reproduced by gracious permission of Her Majesty the Queen.

frequented by game. They know best what suits them. Care should be taken that . . . each covert should lie well to the sun and if possible there should be a stream running through it. Pheasants as well as all animals love warmth and shelter, and in a hard frost they will go any distance for water which is quite necessary for them.'

In conjunction with the clearing of the forest land and the replanting of woodland, the re-routing of streams and formation of lakes and ponds, using the poorer and more difficult ground – generally that most suited to tree planting – the fertile areas favouring crop growing or cattle grazing were also cleared and worked into good heart. What was important was the skilful combining of all such areas on the large scale, to preserve or create an environment favourable to the indigenous wildlife. Our ancestors of the eighteenth and nineteenth centuries, though lacking the help of modern machinery to break up heavy claylands and extensive forests, took into consideration the existing face of the landscape, the direction of prevailing winds, the contours of the ground and the nature of the soil, before they put in hand projects which would substantially affect the existing environment. Many of the wetlands which covered the country in earlier times were drained; this was to the advantage of agriculture and most field sports, though not, of course, to waders and some wildfowl. A new belt of woodland trees could in due course provide a useful windbreak for wintering cattle and, in certain arable areas, it could help to prevent soil erosion, while providing more favourable sanctuaries for game, as well as other fauna and flora.

The extraordinary patchwork of hedgerows and their trees which spans Britain – seen ideally from a vantage-point on a clear day – is derived from the enclosure of land. Early hedgebanks have played a vital role in the mixed arable and stock farming which has continued in the lowlands from the Middle Ages up to the present time. Each hedgebank is in itself a tiny nature reserve, providing cover for many species of wildlife, a rich variety of plants, butterflies and other insects, while also creating sheltered highways connecting one piece of woodland to another which afford protection for all wild creatures. Countryside without hedgerows, where fields are divided by stone walls, wire fences or clean dykes, has a notably less varied population of wild creatures. In 1977 Lord Netherthorpe, a past President of The Game Conservancy said: 'In itself, the shooting man's contribution to habitat improvement and preservation is probably unrivalled by any other group of countrymen'.

People in the landscape

Before we became such an urbanised nation and before the word 'commuter' had been invented, our forefathers spent most of their lives in the country, with the leisure to look around them. Today, most sportsmen either shoot *or* hunt; earlier generations of country people not only shot, hunted and fished, but many individuals were also keen students of natural history. The Victorian era produced a number of first-class amateur ornithologists, lepidopterists and botanists. For example, the sixth Lord Walsingham, one of the finest shots of the latter part of the nineteenth century, was also noted for his studies of rare moths and butterflies, as well as for cataloguing game-bird species and writing two of the famous volumes of the Badminton Library (1887) with Sir Ralph Payne-Gallwey.

It is true that many of the naturalists of the day went in for collections of birds' eggs and butterflies in glass cases – now rightly frowned upon and controlled by legislation. But by and large it was not the neat rows of orange-tips under glass, nor the wooden trays of whitethroat, nightingale or corn bunting's eggs that reduced the wildlife population: although greedy commercial collectors of rare specimens have always been dangerously destructive – and never more so than today – the decline in bird life,

'Old Hardstaff', the keeper, with his pony and his pointers Nelson and Mink. Thomas Edge is shooting partridges in a harvest field on his horse. John Ferneley Snr., dated Melton Mowbray, Leicestershire, 1842.

butterflies and interesting wild plants is largely a result of modern farming methods, the indiscriminate use of chemicals for pest and disease control, and habitat erosion from various causes.

Lord Home, a typical modern example of the all-round sportsman naturalist, describes his feelings about nature in his recent autobiography, *The Way the Wind Blows*:

'Of course, no one who lives close to nature can be wholly starry-eyed, for its ways are also cruel. Both faces of it were known to us as children; for we would watch the stoat hypnotising the rabbit for the kill, the hawk poised for the strike, and the fox stalking its prey. I once met a stoat with its coat completely white, carrying a woodcock in its mouth. Such experiences were a salutary preparation for some of the shocks of life...'

'After living with nature one can never be bored. On many a train journey I have marked the likely pools in a river in which salmon or trout might lie; the field of lucerne or clover where the Clouded Yellow Butterfly might be on the wing in August, and the fields, woods and valleys where the pheasants and partridges might best be driven to test the skill of the guns.'

The scenery of sporting country has always tended to be more alive, visually warmer and more diverse than untended terrain. It is the result of land-owners and tenants avoiding blocks of single crop culture, and ensuring that afforestation follows the natural contours of the land, rather than geometric patterns. In open, flat hunting country – often used for grazing – interest is provided by numerous irregular-shaped copses and fox coverts. On partridge estates, as well as in hunting country, the hedgerows are generally well looked after and sometimes interspersed with attractive trees. Water, too, gives another dimension to the landscape, as, for instance, where it has been dammed to broaden into mill ponds which could be stocked with fish; this is the countryside which Constable and many other artists loved and painted.

Dedham Vale with Ploughmen, *c*1800. John Constable.

'Hunt or be Hunted'. An American Primitive view of the Indian and the buffalo, A bird of prey by J. Snyders.

20

II

The Beginnings of the Hunting Sports

Although the main theme of this book is concerned with the way so many of our rural sports have affected the landscape, it may be of interest, for those who have never had to cope with the problems of a draughty pheasant covert, nor the maintenance of thorn hedges and copses for fox-hunting, nor the care of a chalk stream, to touch briefly upon the way in which the pursuit of quarry gradually evolved from purely primitive needs.

In the early stages of man's development he survived alongside the wild animal populations: sometimes in watchful cohabitation, but more often in conflict. His basic needs included safety from attack, skins for warmth, and some meat to eke out a mainly vegetarian diet. Life in its simplest form was a case of hunt or be hunted.

Early man hunted mainly by craft, using crude but effective weapons and simply contrived pitfalls to trap his quarry. As his skills increased, he added sharpened flints and, later, crude metal weapons and tools to his equipment. In due course such improvements, coupled with a growing sense of fieldcraft, led him to subjugate and train animals which could help with labouring tasks and hunting. When tamed, the wild horse provided strength and speed, and the wild dog and wolf, with their innate intelligence and cunning, would have proved invaluable for hunting and protection.

When cave man hunted and drew pictures

Even in these early times prehistoric man illustrated his hunting with cave paintings and drawings – such was the importance to him of the Chase. The significance of the horse in very early times is demonstrated by the immense silhouettes of horses carved out of the turf on chalk downlands in southern England: the White Horse at Uffington – one of the earliest of the white horse and hill figures of Wessex – is some 374 feet long. It was first recorded in 1084, but was almost certainly a prehistoric cult object (particularly in view of its proximity to an early Iron Age fort).

In many ancient civilisations, both the dog and the horse featured extensively. The horse was always a valuable animal, not only for war, but also for farming and hunting. Civilisations ebbed and flowed across Europe and Asia, and many indigenous strains were brought back and bred into the local stock. Some selective breeding was attempted to develop strains of both horses and dogs for more specific duties. For example, in ancient Egypt and Greece, where competitive sport was a part of everyday life, specially bred Asian and Arab horses were prized for their speed and stamina in both hunting and war.

Among man's earliest weapons was the sling-shot, which, like spears and arrows, could be used either for hunting or self-defence, and against animal or man. The ancient art of falconry, which was developed throughout the Mediterranean lands to take a variety of game birds on the wing, was often accompanied by the bow and arrow. In *The Wildfowler* (1875) Folkard mentions the use in ancient Egypt of the 'throw stick' – not unlike a form of 'boomerang' – which was effectively used against long-necked fowl. The Nile valley with its extensive and luxuriant water course and delta, was always a veritable treasure chest of wildfowl, which could be hunted with little thought being given to numbers or habitat.

By the middle years of the Roman Empire, man had adapted a wide range of creatures to his use. The Romans in particular developed the arts of husbandry and domestication and incidentally introduced to Britain

The White Horse on Milk Hill, Marborough Downs, Wiltshire.

Hunting Fowl with throw stick and greyhounds, from an Egyptian tomb painting.

some game birds and animals which could be maintained as a source of food throughout the seasons. Several mosaic floors of excavated villas show good examples of many animals common to them in Roman times. During their occupation, hunting continued to be a necessary pursuit to provide food: meanwhile ceremonial hunting was often followed by the nobility, either for competition or as a challenging pastime in the open countryside. After the Roman withdrawal around A.D. 400, the Anglo-Saxon nobility tended to revert to the simplest forms of hunting for food rather than sport. By contrast, as the Roman Empire aged, central Rome became more and more concerned with luxury and the trade that flowed from past conquests. Coincidentally with this, their interest in bestial spectator sports increased as their pursuit of game declined and many game species almost disappeared through neglect.

Deer hunting in a wild landscape

The earliest records of any kind of hunting as a challenging sport carried out in an organised manner and supported by horses, hounds and men in Britain go back to A.D. 1079, when the Normans enclosed the area known as the New Forest in the south of England for personal hunting. Soon a further sixty-nine areas of mediaeval forest were brought under the Crown for the deer hunting which the Normans avidly pursued. The scenic benefit to the countryside from this early sport was negligible, but it started the development of the Chase and all that resulted from it. The Norman forest laws, *Carta de Foresta*, which were imposed on an unsophisticated Anglo-

The Vision of St Hubert. Antonio Pisanello, 1425.

Saxon rural society, contained political overtones and were violently unpopular with all classes. The right to hunt deer and to hawk game became conditional on the right to own land and bear arms: both required royal assent, which in the main was granted only to the nobility, who guarded their preserves with strict Game Laws to exclude everybody else.

It was not until the Barons confronted King John that the rural gentry of Britain had sufficient power under the Crown to seize back the hunting rights for their own lands. Even the Game Laws made towards the end of Edward III's reign and after he died in 1377, continued with varying ferocity to protect the privilege of land ownership towards all forms of game and hunting until they were revised early in the nineteenth century. Effectively this precluded most people from participating in the Chase or indeed in any form of game hunting.

During the Crusades, the Plantagenets learnt additional lessons in the arts of venery as they travelled across Europe, and increasingly deer hunting began to revert in England to being a country sport, albeit restricted to nobility and landowners. The Crusaders, while in foreign lands, learnt more about the arts of coursing and falconry, and used their additional knowledge to improve the national methods of hawking on their return.

Hunting wild deer, both on horseback and on foot, was the foremost field sport established in Britain by the end of the fourteenth century. Then as all deer hunting grew more elaborate under the influence of French customs, the less formal hare hunting in the woodlands with packs of the smaller scenting hounds, and hare coursing in the open lands with pairs of fast sighting hounds, continued to rise in popularity among the minor landowners and squires. Both the deer and the hare remained major sources of food, particularly during the winter when farm stock was reserved for the coming season and the people would otherwise have gone almost entirely without fresh meat. The fox, which most people then considered vermin, was kept under control by farmers and landowners hunting on foot with a few slow scenting hounds.

All these forms of hunting required a variety of hounds and sporting dogs. Squire landowners increasingly kept bigger kennels, for the scenting staghounds such as Talbots and Gascons used for deer hunting, the smaller brachet hounds and harriers for hare hunting and the greyhounds and terriers kept for hare coursing, rabbiting, ferreting and other country pursuits. The black and tan Talbots and the blue mottled Gascons were large slow-footed, scenting Southern hounds, which trace their origin back to the first great scenting hounds allegedly bred by St Hubert (A.D. 656–727) – the patron saint of hunting. The Gascony hound in particular formed the backbone of a gentleman's pack for several hundred years, until displaced at the end of the eighteenth century because fox-hunting required the breeding of lighter, faster strains of modern foxhounds.

By the sixteenth century almost a fifth of England was still waste land or virgin forest, much of which was populated by wild deer – both red and fallow – with hares and rabbits in profusion. All forms of hunting and hawking were the main amusements for people of any distinction in the countryside. The lesser nobility were much occupied with building new manor-houses and imparking (by royal assent) much common land, forest

Henry, Prince of Wales (1594–1612) in regal hunting costume drawing his sword for the *coup de grâce* to a stag held by the Earl of Essex. It reflects the Stuarts' enormous interest in hunting and animals. Robert Peake, *c*1610. Reproduced by gracious permission of Her Majesty the Queen.

and open woodland to form private hunting preserves and deer parks. Thus the concept of the larger manorial house and its estate was developing.

The deer was therefore one of the first animals to influence the countryside: the parks where deer could be husbanded became cultivated woodlands, with much attention being paid to existing trees. Often woods were replanted, to the economic advantage of the estate as well as making it visually more attractive. Over the years, deer were hunted by hounds or driven forward to be shot by arrow or crossbow bolt, though the the latter may have generally been used for culling the herd or obtaining carcases for venison.

At the junction of rides created in the woodland, deercotes were built, some of which served the dual purpose of providing winter feeding as well as look-out towers for keepers. Later they were used for observing and culling private herds, but they also produced an architectural embellishment or focal point in the parkland rides. Although deer poaching was a crime punishable by severe penalties, it seems none the less to have provided a challenge for the local people who were not allowed to hunt. Some practical knowledge of the 'art' is evident in Shakespeare's lines from *Titus Andronicus*:

> What! Hast thou not full often struck a doe,
> And borne her cleanly by the Keeper's nose?

Demesnes were generally surrounded by a combination of substantial wooden staked fences and ha-has – ditches and stone walls – to contain the private herd of parked deer. At King's Somborne in Hampshire for example, the original enclosure was surrounded by a twelve-foot-high bank with a deep ditch which wound its way across the landscape. Banks such as these were later incorporated into field or parish boundaries, since they presented formidable barriers to change.

The latter Parks and Forests maintained for deer were referred to as 'These green spots of the King . . . excellent ornament to the beauty of the realm' by Francis Bacon when writing in 1614 of the deer parks. Today Richmond Park, near London, and Windsor Great Park and Forest are two notable reminders of the early enclosed deer parks; they have survived from the time of Henry III, perhaps because they are adjacent to royal residences. Sherwood Forest near Nottingham, Savernake in Wiltshire and

Opposite:
Top left: Deer in Windsor Park. George Barret (1728–84). *Top right:* A view in Richmond Park, Surrey, John Tennant (1796–1872). *Bottom:* Meet of the Royal Buckhounds near Windsor Castle *c*1849. Lord Granville, Master of the Royal Buckhounds, is on the grey and Charles Davis, the huntsman, is in royal livery on the bay. G. H. Laporte (1799–1873).

An imparked estate for deer in the early 18th century. English School.

Hatfield Forest in Hertfordshire are examples of deer forests; they still support some extremely fine examples of old naturally-regenerated forest trees, living reminders of the careful management of the forests of the past. But by the Restoration, the majority of the deer parks had been ruined: trees had been felled, palings pulled down and so many deer killed that a large number were imported from Germany to replenish the depleted stock.

However, deer hunting – both red (stag) and fallow (buck) – recovered in popularity in the mid-seventeenth century and flourished throughout the eighteenth. In time the animals became less wild and were often maintained simply for food and to grace the cultivated wildness of estates fashionable at the time. Sometimes deer were chased around their parks for exercise; great care being taken that they came to no harm, and at the end they were fed a good meal: some were even given nicknames. Carted deer were also chased in the countryside from 1728, but until modern fox-hunting was established in the second half of the eighteenth century, the hare was often the main quest of the Chase for the intervening period of more than a hundred years, and in some areas probably nearer two hundred years. Deer paddock courses, generally a mile in length, were constructed within deer parks for coursing with greyhounds. A type of greyhound for deer coursing was bred specially. Such deerhounds were large and shaggy-coated, standing as high as thirty inches at the shoulder. The courses contained pens for the deer and kennels for the dogs, and were encompassed with pales, behind which the spectators and judges sat. Courses were run for plates and money; the whole scene resembled the early gatherings for horse racing. Blaine's *Encyclopaedia of Rural Sport* describes such a meeting: 'At Cowdrey in Sussex, the seat of Lord Montecute A.D. 1591, one day after dinner The Queen saw from a turret sixteen bucks all having *fayre lawe*, coursed with greyhounds on a lawn'.

In time, the herds of wild red deer began to decline in the more cultivated areas of the English lowlands: not only were they killed because of their general destructiveness in the open woodlands, but their habitat was restricted because of extensive forest clearance throughout the countryside. Both the wild red and fallow deer became increasingly concentrated in the lightly-wooded and poor acid heathland soils of the New Forest in Hampshire, and parts of Exmoor in Devon. The few red deer found in Norfolk are descended from carted escapees from the Norwich staghounds, and those in the Pennine uplands from park escapees.

Today, the now unwooded moorland heaths, like Exmoor, are jealously guarded from the incursion of private farming as areas of great historic value and wild scenic beauty. How long these sanctuaries of red deer will remain is uncertain – they are relics of a bygone age of hunting – and it is now in the Highlands of Scotland that this, the largest, and arguably the most beautiful, of all wild animals in the British Isles has its last real stronghold on the bare mountain slopes.

Fallow deer were maintained in a number of parked estates – for instance Windsor Park, where the park and the surrounding forest provided a large enough area for buckhunting – and the bucks were hunted with a pack of hounds 'encouraged' solely to this form of hunting. This sport was continued in England throughout the nineteenth century on Exmoor, in the New Forest, in Lancashire, Devon and Somerset.

Brook Hawking, from Richard Blome's *The Gentleman's Recreation.*

Falconry or Hawking – the sport of hunting flying game

The history of hawking in England probably goes back to the seventh or eighth century, but the actual dates are not clear. Hawking certainly seems to have been practised earlier in northern Europe than in Britain, perhaps as early as A.D. 480 – it is covered by the Ripuarian Code of laws, transcribed and compiled between the reigns of Clovis and Dagobert over northern France from 480 to 620. Our words 'hawk' and 'hawking' certainly have older European equivalents. Falconry was indeed practised in the ancient civilisations of Egypt, the Roman Empire and Japan, but the sport as we know it evolved from the methods of falconry which came to Britain by way of Europe from Asia Minor and Arabia. Towards the end of the eleventh century, hawking had become popular both as a rural sport and a social grace, and all persons of any standing aimed to become proficient at it. By the beginning of the thirteenth century it was a widely practised art, as shown in this extract from Blaine's *Encyclopaedia of Rural Sports*:

'The assumption of the throne of England by William the Conqueror, a monarch passionately fond of field sports, tended greatly to the advancement of the hawking mania, as well as to increase the severity of the laws for the preservation of game of all kinds. . . None but persons of the highest rank were even allowed to be in possession of a hawk, nor was it until the *Carta de Foresta* had been forced from King John by the "barons bold", that every free man was privileged to have eyeries of hawks, falcons and eagles in his own woods, with heronries also. The oppressive nature of the laws relating to this sport, notwithstanding this concession, continued to be felt during several successive reigns. In the 34th [year] of Edward the Third, it was made felony to steal a hawk; to take its eggs even in a person's own grounds, was punishable with imprisonment for a year and a day, besides subjecting the offender to a fine, at the king's pleasure.

'During many centuries hawking appears to have been the all-absorbing pursuit, not only in England, but equally so throughout Europe; indeed, it might be said that a hawking mania then raged universally. Kings and princes not only engaged in the actual chase itself, but they also voluntarily undertook the drudgery of training and feeding their hawks themselves. When employed in their most important offices, they were often seen with a hawk on their hand: indeed, they seldom moved without them, their hawks being apparently considered as much their familiar acquaintances and attendants, as pet dogs are with us of the present day. King Stephen also, like Harold, is almost invariably portrayed with his favourite bird resting on his hand. Even Archbishop Becket could not go to the French court or an embassy without his hawks and falconers. . . Edward the Third, according to Froissart, had with him, when he invaded France, thirty falconers on horseback, who had the charge of his falcons.'

The fourteenth century saw the enthusiastic development of hawking in England, led by royalty and the nobility. It was a sport which provided the fascination of the Chase, though carried on in the sky with flying game; even magpies and crows were acceptable quarry during the closed season from Easter until the corn was cut. Queen Elizabeth I patronised the sport, as had all her forebears, but its popularity waned during the reign of James

I and languished under the shadow of Cromwell. Towards the latter half of the eighteenth century, there was a partial revival.

A large variety of hawks and falcons was kept by the nobility and each bird was supposed to have been graded to the owner's rank. Though this belief is stated in many books, it is apparently based on a fanciful listing in the *Boke of St Albans*, and therefore has no basis in fact. At all events the peregrine soon became by far the most important falcon, as it could be flown at plover, snipe, pigeon, duck, grouse and pheasant, as well as at herons and gulls. Falcons were generally not flown at fur or ground game for fear of damaging their wing or tail feathers. The long-winged 'falcons' such as the peregrine fly out wide and high, and it is in the open sky, with

A hawking party, accompanied by great ceremonial in a large clearing with wooded surroundings. John Wootton.

A heron-hawking party with spaniels – from *The National Sports of Great Britain*, 1821. Henry Alken Snr.

the benefit of height and great speed, that they make their 'stoop' (the rapid descent of a falcon from a height onto a flying quarry – sometimes also 'swoop', as in Macbeth's 'at one fell swoop'). 'Hawks', such as the goshawk, are shorter-winged and fly at their prey to strike it near the ground. The only short-winged hawks used by falconers in Europe were the goshawk and the sparrow-hawk; both the male and female of the former and generally the female of the latter. The goshawk was used in Britain chiefly in the enclosed country of hedgerows and open woodlands – where it would be impossible to fly a falcon – against rabbits, hares and pheasants.

The short-winged hawks were termed 'hawks of the fist' because they flew from the fist at their quarry, not stooping from a height, as do the falcons. They were trained to return to the fist, where they were accustomed to feed. The long-winged falcons were called 'hawks of the lure' because they were trained to fly back to the lure when necessary.

Pigeons were popular for training young hawks, but once 'entered' to them problems could arise where neighbouring estates maintained dove-cots. Hawks were seldom entered to more than a few species of quarry; the more they were kept at a particular type of game the better they would fly it – not being distracted once the chase was joined, which explains why the

mews of most falconers often contained a wide variety of birds to suit differing quarry.

Hawking parties were followed on horseback with footmen to assist; spaniels and pointers were generally used to drive out or find the game in cover: it could be quite a lengthy procedure to set up a hawking party with a number of hawks and falcons and take them out into stretches of countryside frequented by game, particularly as the weather was an important factor. Heron hawking with falcons was a popular sport for hawking parties, as the Chase would often be met several hundred feet up in the air, and the larger birds were easy to see and follow over quite long distances.

Complete mobility and open spaces were required for falconry, and as the countryside became more enclosed, the sport declined. Although it may be said to have had little or no effect on the landscape – because of the open uninterrupted space preferred – it was an important first stage in the development of hunting flying game.

The stalking horse, much used by early fowlers. From *The Gentleman's Recreation*.

There was little in the way of game shooting in the fifteenth century, since the early military weapons could hardly be developed for sport. However, there were the longbow and the crossbow: the latter was developed principally by the militia, and became lighter as it evolved, so that it could also be used as a sporting weapon. Greyhounds were sometimes used for the sighted retrieval of wounded quarry. The new ease of hunting with a crossbow freed gentlemen for the first time to go out for food and sport without a retinue.

By the middle of the sixteenth century, the crossbow and the hawk had been joined by the fowling gun for hunting game birds. Early fowlers used two methods, 'enchantment' and 'enticement'; with the former the fowl was drawn to the sportsman by whistle or call, with the latter it was wooed by 'machines' or 'engines' so that it became entangled in nets unawares. A large number of devices and hides was also designed to shield the hunter from view. Even in those early times, as *The Sportsman's Dictionary* (1735) pointed out:

'. . . waterfowl are in their own nature the most subtile and cunning of birds, and the most careful for their own safety; hence they have been compared to an orderly and well governed camp, having scouts on land afar off, courts of guards, sentinels, and all sorts of other watchful officers to give an alarm of the approach of any seeming danger.'

Gervase Markham's *Hunger's Prevention – The Whole Art of Fowling by Water and Land*, published in 1621, illustrates the importance of fowling as a means of procuring food; wildfowl have always been an esteemed luxury, because their flesh was thought to be more wholesome and easier to digest than that of tame fowls. At that time his advice was to 'shoot game on the ground; as many as possible with one shot'. Stalking horses were also employed to get to close quarters with the birds. Even 'stalking deer' formed out of painted canvas with natural horns attached could be used for fowl familiar with stalking horses, where deer often fed. Netting, using a variety of methods, was also part of fowling. The three methods of shooting, stalking and netting gradually came into use by country squires, who could hunt alone or with a servant, to take game birds for the table. On more festive occasions small family gatherings of local landowners would go out to enjoy themselves on horseback, accompanied by their staff.

Fowling guns towards the end of the sixteenth century were just reaching a degree of development making it possible to kill, or incapacitate and gather with dogs, a variety of wildfowl and other game: duck, partridge, woodcock, pheasant, snipe, swan, goose, heron, bittern, plover and fieldfare (all of which were valued for their meat and flavour in those days). Fowling guns with the following actions – match-locks (*c*1450), wheel locks (1500–1700), snaphaunce (*c*1580) and flint-locks (1600–1900) – often with barrels as long as fifty-four inches were in use. Many were imported from Europe. Sportsmen often had several different guns of various types and sizes. The flint-lock guns, shooting a more regular tumbled shot instead of small hand-rounded lumps of lead, had become a new sporting weapon for the English squire, ousting the crossbow which – perhaps owing to its

Sir Edward Hales. A superb portrait full of detail. The flintlock has the very long barrel of the day. Philippe Mercier, dated 1744.

quietness and handiness – none the less lingered on as a weapon for poaching. Shooting became established as the sport for taking game birds, alongside hawking.

However, all early muzzle-loading guns were unwieldy, being long and badly balanced, difficult to reload and subject to many misfires and hang-fires so that few shots were got off in a day. Most of these taken by stalking the quarry to close quarters and then generally shooting at game birds on the ground or on water. It was a difficult and cumbersome business, and reloading in damp weather was almost impossible.

The close of the 16th century and change

Queen Elizabeth I had been an ardent supporter of the Chase and had been responsible for improvements to many country sports during her reign: by the close of the sixteenth century they were widely established. National attitudes to the Chase were still significantly different in Britain and Europe. For the French and Germans, the hunt was a spectacle to be enjoyed only by persons of noble birth, and the ceremonial of the kill was an important climax, whereas in Britain the skill involved in hunting was considered more important. This attitude affected the social status of field sports: hunting in Britain was a recreation for the country community, probably headed by the squire, and enjoyed by his huntsmen, yeomen and visitors alike, and the kill was no more than a logical end to the fieldcraft employed in the Chase.

Early fox-hunting

Some first records of fox-hunting date from the middle of the sixteenth century, when the attitude to this form of 'vermin hunting' was still luke-warm. More often than not, it was prompted by a desire to prevent the

The Duke of Marlborough's 'Craftsman'. John Wootton, c1820.

destruction of lambs and poultry which were being husbanded, and the fox was killed by setting baited traps and snares, or shot. Foxes were generally hunted on foot, starting at dawn when the scent was strong and the fox was slow. The hunt often ended with the fox going to ground, only to be bolted by terriers or dug out and knocked on the head. This was termed 'hunting below ground'; the newer 'hunting above ground', illustrated in Richard Blome's edition of *The Gentleman's Recreation* (1686), was altogether a more mobile sport and took people out into the wide open spaces like hare hunting had done.

Horse breeding and racing

The heavy, ponderous horses used for the ceremonial of stag hunting underwent considerable refinement by the introduction of Arab blood lines and selective breeding methods, which brought an infusion of speed and mobility into sport. The Newmarket gallops and a racecourse were established at the beginning of the seventeenth century, under the auspices of James I, for the promotion of horseracing as a necessary and vital test for improving the breed. In 1616 the Monarch purchased the Markham Arabian for the royal stables as a stud horse to improve the English stock. It had been found in Europe that Arab horses possessed excellent qualities and also bred true. Horses were in increasing demand by the military to provide greater mobility, and also by the growing country squirearchy, who did most of their travelling on horseback in the days of cart tracks and unsurfaced highways. Early races were often challenges between two or more horses for wagers between owners to compare performance as a guide to breeding lines. Good racecourses were established at many country towns and even in London at Hyde Park (land which originally belonged to Westminster Abbey and was taken over by Henry VIII at the time of the dissolution of the monasteries in 1536–39). Race meetings were banned during the Commonwealth of Cromwell as being opportunities for the seditious to gather. All sport was in one way or another affected during this time.

Coursing. J. Barenger (1780–1831), dated 1811.

Coursing

Hounds and sporting dogs also became more uniform and fleeter as a result of being bred selectively for their special activities, and the strains were more carefully maintained by planned breeding, in place of previous haphazard matings. Hare coursing with pairs of greyhounds by sight began to be segregated from the popular hare hunting by scent. A definitive code for coursing was established by the Duke of Norfolk on instructions from Queen Elizabeth I, and subscribed to by the chief gentry. Park deer, forest deer and foxes were also coursed with greyhounds at this time. A description appears in an entry in *The Sportsman's Dictionary* (1735):

'Coursing with greyhounds, is a recreation in great esteem with many gentlemen. It affords greater pleasure than hunting in some respects. As firstly, because it is sooner ended. Secondly it does not require much toil. Thirdly the game is for the most part always in sight. Fourthly in regard to the delicate qualities and shape of the greyhound.'

The entry further describes how, when coursing park deer in a paddock course, a terrier was required to drive away the deer before the greyhounds were slipped – usually a brace and never more than two brace. Forest deer were coursed either from wood to wood, or on the lawns and fields around the keepers' lodges: young hounds were thrown into cover to drive out the deer, then the greyhounds were slipped if the deer was suitable for coursing.

But it was the popular hare coursing for competition between owners and breeders with matched pairs of greyhounds, carried out under judges with rules, that was the commoner sport in the countryside. One of the early rules laid down that the hare should normally be given 'twelve score yards' (240 yards) before the greyhounds were slipped; in Mr Thacker's amended rules *c*1820 this became four to five score yards.

It appears that the principles of coursing at this time were not really very different from those existing around A.D. 150 in England. But the sport

A kill at Ashdown Park, Berkshire. Greyhounds course their hare while a shepherd watches his flock. James Seymour, dated 1743.

37

seems to have started much earlier in the Middle Eastern countries where the long dog or greyhound's initial function must have been one of food procurement. It may well have preceded falconry, but, as both seem to have been practised in the middle dynasties of Egyptian civilisation, it is difficult to ascertain. Like falconry, coursing brought about no change to the landscape or its vegetation as it, too, needed large open areas; but as one would expect, coursing was also badly affected by the enclosure of land.

Fowling and shooting

Flint-locks, more than any other type were steadily developed over the next two centuries and the art of shooting flying became more feasible as improvements were made to guns and ammunition, and the whole process of firing became faster. However, although new and more efficient designs and systems were being perfected all the time, shooting flying only made slow progress in the seventeenth century, as it required the best guns available, which were scarce and enjoyed by few sportsmen. Gun dogs were often essential for recovering such game as had been slightly wounded by the relatively few lead pellets used at this time in the shot charge; whereas today an average game cartridge would contain about three hundred even pellets with generally more than half remaining in the target area up to forty yards, probably less than fifty hail-shot pellets would then have been used. A loader or a servant was needed to carry the charging equipment and to assist in loading the weapons.

Below left: The Day's Sport. The bag includes pheasant, partridge, woodcock, swan, hare, snipe, turnstones and mallard. James Ward, dated 1826. *Right, top*: Warreners ferreting rabbits (detail). Richard Ansdell; *centre*: Black-neck pheasant. Charles Whymper, *c*1890; *below*: Ringneck pheasant. E. J. Amoore, dated 1902.

The gentry, who for centuries had been preserving wild deer and breeding park deer, were now concerned to husband their partridges, pheasants, wildfowl and duck for both hawking and shooting – in fact all their edible game, which was of considerable economic importance to the household, as well as for the sport it provided. New English Game Laws introduced by Parliament in 1671 limited the 'taking of game' only to those holding a freehold estate with rentals of more than £100 per annum, a leasehold estate for ninety-nine years of £150 per year, and to the eldest son or heir of an esquire or person of superior rank. This effectively debarred most yeomen from shooting, which had now become considerably easier than hawking. Other laws proliferated, relating to the appointment of keepers, the ownership of sporting dogs, possessing game and so on.

A great impetus was given to shooting flying by the ending of the Commonwealth in 1660, as many noblemen and cavaliers returned from exile in Europe where they had witnessed this new form of sport being carried out. By this time also the flint-lock had been steadily developed for more than fifty years. In 1686, Richard Blome in his *Gentleman's Recreation* gave advice to hunters with regard to shooting 'flying': 'It is the best and surest way, for when your game is on the wing it is more exposed to danger. . . .' Although he could not have realised it at the time, the impact of shooting flying was to inspire as much care and attention to the countryside as the creation of the deer preserves had in earlier times.

Game reserves become sporting demesnes

The need to hunt primarily for food gradually became less important as manors and villages organised their resources better. Animal husbandry and breeding was generally beginning to be more widely understood, and the salting of winter meat was often carried out. Manorial estates started to build a variety of reserves for food. Dovecots were built for pigeon, yards made for poultry and decoys for waterfowl. Country folk also hawked and netted partridges and ferreted rabbits from warrens; both were plentiful and contributed to a supply of fresh meat during the winter months.

Fishing as a sport was resurrected during the sixteenth century, bringing with it a more sophisticated approach to methods. Skills developed over many years in the early stew ponds were transferred to streams and rivers, which resulted in their being cleared and often improved. Mill ponds, created for water power to grind corn, were also carefully husbanded for the fishing.

From the harvesting of game as additional fresh food, a progressive attitude to the manorial estate began to emerge – with its wide variety of field sports, agriculture and animal husbandry – and with it a changing landscape, in part moulded to assist the newer forms of hunting.

The origins and history of the pheasant

Of all our country sports, shooting probably effected the greatest visual impact on the landscape because of the extensive planting and management of cover that was undertaken to provide game habitat. And of all the quarry species involved, it must surely be the pheasant that has been the cause of

Pheasant shooting with spaniels in rough open ground before the leaf-fall. William Jones (*fl.* 1832–54).

the most spectacular changes. Partridges, grouse, wildfowl, deer, foxes and fish all had in their own ways come to influence our rural scenery, but the varied habitat created for pheasants is the easiest to see and appreciate. Some of the attractive features which can be credited to the requirements of pheasant management include magnificent hill-top coverts, scattered woodlands and insignificant copses; a farm spared from block-cropping by diverse stands of kale, maize or sunflowers; or even a small reedbed saved from draining.

We shall never be quite certain when the pheasant reached our shores, but fossils of *phasianidae* from the Miocene period – along with ibis-like water birds, ducks and pelicans – have been found in France and could easily have occurred in Great Britain. Many species of pheasants were known to have existed in China in antiquity. An ancient Chinese character

Pheasant shooting with spaniels in a woodland clearing by a stream. Sam Alken.

which means 'pheasant' was certainly used during the Shang or Yin Dynasty (the traditional date for the end of this dynasty is 1027 B.C.). Some of the pheasant species recognised much later during the T'ang Dynasty (A.D. 618–889), are listed in *The Golden Peaches of Samarkand* by Edward Schafer. Among them is the Reeves pheasant which was 'indigenous to North China and since the dim and glorious past has lent its flaunting plumes to ceremonial and military artists for wands, standards, and hats . . . for courtly fans and for the most elegant parasols'.

In western Europe pheasants were first described by classical Greek writers such as Aeschylus, who mentioned that they lived along the banks of the River Phasis in the land then called Colchis (hence the scientific name *Phasianus c. colchicus*). Colchis is now the Soviet Republic State of Georgia, and the modern name for the river is the Rioni. The Reverend H. A. Macpherson said of this region 'forests and marshes fringed the shallow and slimey waters of the slow-flowing Rioni' (*The Pheasant*, Fur and Feather Series). There is also mention of pheasants in the fable of the Argonauts, who set out from Greece to search for the Golden Fleece on the eastern shores of the Black Sea. While the Argonauts' expedition is recorded as myth, even the most hardened sceptics think that the legend must have been based on fact: the events probably took place in the thirteenth century B.C. As to the Golden Fleece, in those days alluvial gold is believed to have been collected by the natives on fleeces laid on the river bed, the earliest form of placer mining (*see* Robert Graves' *The Greek Myths*, Volume 2).

Ring-neck pheasant. Rodger McPhail.

Buffon's *Natural History* (written 1771, this edition 1812) describes the capture of pheasants by the Argonauts thus: 'That bold body of adventurers saw in ascending the Phasis these beautiful birds scattered along its banks; they carried them home to Greece, and in doing so, they conferred a richer present than that of the golden fleece'. One wonders how the pheasants survived the journey. The open galley *Argo* was said to have been a fifty-oared fighting ship, not a roomy sailing vessel; Jason would not have wanted to be completely dependent on the winds like a merchantman under sail and would have had to defend himself from attack; finally, the return journey from Colchis was probably made via the coast of south Russia, where they would have run into ice floes, as described in Lionel Casson's *The Ancient Mariners*. None the less somehow *Phasianus colchicus* did eventually turn up in Greece, and in due course some birds were taken to Rome. We know that by the middle of the first century A.D. pheasant was appreciated as a table bird, and had become part of the livestock of the wealthier Roman villa. This phasian bird is the species we now call the Old English Black-neck.

Buffon also tells us that from the land of Colchis 'they spread eastward through Media', now north-west Iran. In fact the black-necked pheasant, or a closely related species, inhabited many parts of what used to be called Asia Minor, including northern Greece, Turkey and Bulgaria, and it remains there to this day, though in Bulgaria the native stock has hybridised with imported Ring-necks, which the local game experts are now trying to weed out.

When one of the authors of this book was working on a pheasant project on the shores of the Caspian in Iran – perhaps only four hundred miles from the original Colchis discoveries – he was interested to examine specimens of the native pheasant *Phasianus colchicus talischensis*. It was small, black-necked and in many ways not unlike a nippy little version of our gamekeeper's favourite, the Old English. The more correct name for this particular species is in fact the South Caucasian Black-neck. Further along the Caspian to the east the native bird is *Phasianus colchicus persicus*, again fairly similar in appearance.

Several writers have suggested that the Phoenicians – setting sail from around Tyre and Sidon – might have brought the pheasant to England. Some years ago, Robert Graves, the scholar, was asked whether he considered that the maritime Phoenicians (or Sidonians, as they called themselves) would have bothered with pheasants. He thought it very unlikely, as they were mostly traders, not true settlers, who dealt in manufactured goods such as jewellery, glass and metalwork, which they would have exchanged for pearls, gold, tin and copper. They did, of course, plant vineyards in southern France, and by 1,000 B.C. had established other colonial trading posts along the Mediterranean – an extensive one at Utica,

not far from the Tunis of today, and later another one beyond the Straits of Gibraltar near Cadiz.

Recent archaeological research suggests that the evidence that the pheasant reached Britain in prehistoric times is rather slight, although other seafaring colonists had been visiting Britain from about 2,500 B.C. – bringing with them cattle, sheep and corn. The first, often quoted, mention

of the pheasant in England was apparently in A.D. 1059, when the bird was recorded on what might be called a list of rations for a Canon's household, drawn up by King Harold; in this list, two partridges are given as the alternative to one pheasant. It is unlikely that the Saxons or Danes would have introduced exotic birds and animals, and there is no reliable evidence that they did; nor were the Normans any more likely to have done so. It seems, therefore, that the pheasant must have been brought to Britain considerably earlier with Roman officers on foreign garrison duty, towards the end of their colonial period. We know that they introduced fallow deer; and we also know that the pheasant had for some time been a part of villa life, maintained, like the peacock, to eat as well as admire. So it seems logical to assume that they would have had pheasants around them too. Palladius, a Roman writer of the fourth century A.D., dealt at some length with the management of pheasants as domestic fowl in captivity, and included cures for the disease of gapes which were in use until quite recently.

Roman merchants and officials are known to have crossed the Channel regularly from Boulogne to Richborough and Dover to London. They also crossed from the Garonne, the Loire and the Seine estuaries – a comparatively short journey for a crate full of pheasants. Although their ships did not venture far during the winter months, their vessels were by that time quite sizeable and seaworthy.

Various early diarists recorded eating meals of pheasant. It is said that Thomas Becket, Archbishop of Canterbury, dined off pheasant with great relish on the last night of his life, December 29th, 1170, before being put to death by Henry II's knights. But it was a rather rare game bird and provided delicate meat in the winter months.

In the sixteenth century there was a royal game preserve around London which extended from Westminster to St Giles-in-the-Fields, and thence to Islington, Hampstead, Highgate and Hornsey Park. Henry VIII was a great sportsman and it is only reasonable to suppose that he flew his hawks at pheasants which had been reared and put out into the coverts.

By the eighteenth century other species were introduced to follow up the original black-necks from their far-away Caucasian riverbeds. Although no record of the Chinese pheasant, *Ph. c. torquatus*, appears until 1768 (in Thomas Pennant's *British Zoology*), Eric Parker – then editor of *The Field* – described some mosaics taken from a Roman villa built *c*A.D. 300 near Carthage which illustrated villa life in detail. The scene included two pheasants, one a Black-neck and 'the other plainly *torquatus*, the Ring-neck'. So by that time the Romans were certainly keeping Ring-necks, though whether they brought them over to England is another matter.

However, only a few years ago another Roman mosaic, depicting a ring-necked species was uncovered at Woodchester in Gloucestershire, the site of a Roman villa thought to date from the fourth century. So the 1768 introduction of ring-necks may not have been the first. It is possible that, as the tea trade opened up with China, the clippers brought with them new consignments of birds. One wonders what percentage survived the sixteen thousand mile voyage from Shanghai to London, which took approximately a hundred days.

The Chinese pheasant is only one of the ring-necked species – there are seventeen in this category which is classified as the grey-rumped group – an ugly-sounding name for such beautiful birds. The rather similar Formosan pheasant is another that has been introduced to this country. The fast-flying Reeves pheasant (*Syrmaticus reeves*), a bird of woodland rather than arable habitat, was imported from China about 1831.

In 1840 the first Japanese Green pheasants (*Phasianus versicolor*) were brought to Amsterdam; one pair from this consignment, according to Tegetmeir, passing into the possession of Lord Derby. Shortly after this, some of the progeny were acquired by the Gurney family of Norfolk; this stock was used for the coverts rather than for aviary purposes. Later on, others were imported from Japan and by 1860 the species was well established in Europe. Not many years ago, The Game Conservancy was experimenting with this breed in areas of heavy rainfall, because Green pheasants survive well in their native land where the rainfall can be up to a hundred inches a year, much of it falling in the breeding season. The pure-bred Japanese Green is somewhat smaller than most of the other game species.

In 1900 the so-called Mongolian birds (*Ph. c. mongolicus*) were brought over by Lord Rothschild. These birds are really Kirghiz pheasants, and are not found in any part of Mongolia. They inhabit the land between the Aral Sea and the north-western parts of Chinese Turkestan.

The beautiful melanistic pheasant (*Ph. c. mut. tenebrosus*) is not a species with a geographical origin, but a mutation which eventually became established. Odd specimens were first noticed by Lord Rothschild in Norfolk game dealers' shops about 1880, but not classified until 1927 after considerable study by the Japanese ornithologist Hachisuka.

The Evolution of Farming and Forestry

Having outlined the gradual development of hunting, we can now look at the backcloth against which this took place. Early settlers in Britain, from Bronze Age man to the Romans and Saxons, were naturally drawn to the lighter soils that they were capable of working with their simple implements. Thus large tracts of land with heavy clay soils remained afforested, as in prehistoric times, while the lighter soils supported a more open woodland combined with some pasture. Many unworkable areas remained covered with heathland, bog or scrub.

In the earliest farming colonies, grain was grown and farm animals husbanded, so that small communities were self-supporting on the lands they worked. Some of the lighter, open forest was cleared for crop growing by the Romans and later by the Saxons, although the latter tended to move on once the soil had been exhausted by repetitive farming.

In areas of the country where the poor soils were generally unable to sustain a farming community, hunting and trapping were frequently the only source of food in wintertime. Rabbits, which often colonised the lighter, poorer soils, were a common source of meat, but were never considered to be game animals.

By the start of the Middle Ages, a desire to grow more than the community needed for its support released energies which led to some simple drainage schemes being tackled and wetlands cleared for cultivation or grazing. Sheep and goats – often the primary farm animals of earlier periods on thinner soils – were also great reclamators, converting scrubland to pasture, but man still had to make clearings in the established forest to enlarge the enclosed and farmed acreage and also provide firewood and hurdles for stock fences.

The Age of timber

It is difficult nowadays to realise the importance of timber – particularly oak – in those early times: trees were in endless demand for building timber-framed houses, and for making furniture, wagons and carriages,

Landscape near Linkenholt, Hampshire.

agricultural implements and tools. The great need for timber in a developing agricultural society led to a steady and continuing destruction of our native forest lands which had until that time been sufficiently self-regenerating. John Evelyn, the diarist, noted in 1662 that '... waste and destruction of our woods has been universal', and he was not alone in his concern about the trend towards widespread deforestation and the reduction of woodlands at that time. He called for responsible people to undertake extensive replanting to replace the disappearing woodlands. And indeed in the late seventeenth century new systems of cropping without replanting were developed; of these, the coppice-with-standards method and pollarding were popular. Generally this required a planting of indigenous oak, interspersed with hornbeam, hazel, chestnut or ash; the new growth from coppiced trees was cut down to the root bole, while the pollarded bole was left high enough to prevent damage to the new shoots by browsing animals. Careful cutting and rotation provided materials for fencing, tools, wheels, rural implements and fuel. The Forest of Dean for example was re-afforested in 1680, the twentieth year of Charles II's reign, following an Act of Parliament. 'Regarders' – officers of the King's Forest – were also appointed to oversee offences or defaults committed by the foresters, or within the forest boundaries.

With the enclosure of land by quickthorn hedges, it became normal to intersperse the quickthorn with oak, elm or ash which was allowed to grow to maturity and provided shade and shelter for the cattle that mixed farming required, as well as straight timber. In this way one of the many attractive and characteristic aspects of the traditional English landscape was created.

As Britain became a seafaring nation, requirements for oak again increased substantially: for example a man-of-war of 1785, like Nelson's *Agamemnon* of sixty-four guns, needed some three thousand tons of mature oaks for its construction – perhaps sixty acres of trees. There was a parallel demand for the other indigenous timbers such as elm for the keels, also ash and beech. As the need for charcoal for iron smelting and glassblowing increased, further inroads were made into the hardwoods, so that demand finally began to outstrip the natural supply from both the regenerating woodlands and the oak forests planted near the centres of shipbuilding and elsewhere. As a result some timber had to be imported.

All this was but an early exercise for the massive replanting of woodlands which took place throughout the eighteenth and nineteenth centuries, many of them the woodlands which we now admire for their form and variety. A large number of the old winding thorn hedges remaining today has become widely intermixed over the centuries, with other species such as crab apple, damson, maple and hazel, and the wild rose. As shown in *Hedges* by Pollard, Hooper and Moore, recent studies of hedge species have made it possible to age hedges on different soils and in different regions by a count of the varieties; their calculations show an approximate dating of one hundred years of age for each specie in a thirty yard stretch of hedge. Some of the older hedgebanks are parish or county boundaries going back hundreds of years; others were practical divisions of land into shapes workable by man and his horses; yet others followed the old drove roads and the easy contours of the land..

Climate and soil

Climate and soil have naturally played an influential role in the development of farming, by determining the prosperity of the individual communities, the type of crops produced by them, and thus the pattern of the landscape and its development. In Wessex, for example, which has large areas of both chalkland and clayland, two distinct patterns emerged. In the chalklands of southern Wiltshire, Dorset and most of northern Hampshire, sheep and corn have dominated the farming scene from early times to the present day. In the claylands of northern Wiltshire and Dorset and parts of Somerset, however, local farming has concentrated on cattle and pig rearing and dairy produce. In the two areas of Wiltshire the distinction between chalk, and clay or 'cheese' country, is underlined by the saying 'as different as chalk and cheese'.

The old farming practices

Crop farming before the enclosures – whether enforced by Parliament or privately agreed – was generally arranged on the 'open or common field system'. This system was developed around a manorial or village community as the countryside was opened up, and was based on communal farming, embracing both areas of common grazing, often with sheep and cattle which were jointly owned, and parcels of individual crop tillage laid out in strips of different ownership. The long strips of ploughland, often up to a chain wide and perhaps a furlong in length, were cropped individually and separated by narrow, unproductive paths between, which, as soil was ploughed to the middle of the strips, often assisted the drainage. Some

Farming at Woburn, Bedfordshire c1750. The planted hedgerows have the 'popple' look produced by the many round-headed standards not yet laid to strengthen the hedges for cattle. George Lambert.

evidence of this early kind of farming can still be seen in the many corrugated fields around the Midlands. Another legacy of this system of land division is the grazing furlong, separated by hedges a chain or two apart. The open field system of sixteenth century Britain can still be seen – and still functions – on land at Laxton in Nottinghamshire. An example of a similar feudal system can be witnessed in France in the Bordeaux (Aquitaine) region today, where peasant farmers crop rows of vines, although the various rows within a *clos* may be separated from one another and intermingled with those of other owners.

The open field system played a useful role in the development of farming, but it was inefficient and incapable of providing sufficient grain for a growing population. It was particularly anomalous in the best corngrowing areas of the Midlands, East Anglia and parts of Wessex until the parliamentary Enclosure Act of George II created larger units which were

The Reapers. Enamel on Wedgwood biscuit earthenware. George Stubbs, 1795.

divided by the commissioners into rectangular-shaped fields of single ownership. However, people in some parts of the country, particularly in the south of England, had agreed amongst themselves to redistribute land into much larger fields of single ownership to form family farm units by local agreements long before the enclosures were enforced. This happened in the prosperous Cotswolds, where the early wool trade from the enormous herds of downland sheep flourished during the Middle Ages; here a hunting man, not yet understanding the need for jumping, might ride out very much where he pleased.

The enclosures

There are no accurate and complete records of the enclosures. As they did not have the same effect in all areas they often meant different things to different people, but everywhere feelings ran high. Much land was enclosed towards the end of the seventeenth century – mainly in the better soil regions as yet unfarmed – and the enclosures continued into the early part of the nineteenth century. They provided the impetus for a revolution in farming and stockbreeding methods which in time embraced nearly seven million acres of previously uncultivated waste, wood and scrubland. The later enclosures were essentially regular in appearance, with hedges running generally north–south and east–west, sometimes creating wedge-shaped fields when incorporating existing roads or old boundaries in their perimeter.

The enclosures with their surrounding hedges were to have a beneficial effect on both game shooting and hunting as the countryside became more manageable. Some counties, like Oxfordshire, were enclosed to a third of their area, others more, and some hardly at all. Scrubland was generally enclosed into fields of ten acres or so for arable farming, but in the grasslands of the Midlands the fields were of far larger sizes owing to the

An English landscape with varied crops and hedged fields – hunted over and cared for – as opposed to the bleak deserts of monoculture where there is little wildlife.

The Essex Hunt. The scene shows the effects of Enclosure by hedgerow in open country, again with the early 'popple' appearance of small trees interspersed alongside a coppiced woodland covert – hunting country. Dean Wolstenholme Snr., dated 1830.

landownership of big estates. Trevelyan wrote: 'The Enclosure movement was a necessary step to feed the increasing population, and it increased not only the wealth of the landlords who put money into their estates, but that of the large tenant farmers who were their principal agents in the movement'.

As enclosure got under way, the lack of woodlands was still being debated, and the partition of the open country by the Commissioners' rectangular grid lines was seen by some to be destructive of the 'beautiful wild scenery'. However, it was businesslike, if somewhat over-regimented. As the hedges were planted, thousands of miles of drainage ditches were dug, and in the many corners of land produced by the new order of straightness small sanctuaries for game began to regenerate. In time the countryside took on the appearance of a chessboard pattern of innumerable fields enclosed by hedges and stone walls. William Marshall wrote of the late eighteenth-century landscape: 'The enclosures are small, and the hedges high and full of trees. This has a singular effect in travelling through the country: the eye seems ever on the verge of a forest, which is, as it were by enchantment, continually changing into inclosures and hedgerows'.

The Harvest of 1857. This picture in the Yale Center for British Art is accompanied by the farm record book, so that the crops in most of the fields can be identified – shooting country. John Frederick Herring Snr.

The influence of changes in farming

Farming in Britain has undergone many alterations since the 1650s, not only caused by changes in ownership and methods, but also resulting from the external pressures of urban industrialisation, with the growth of transport systems throughout the country and the increase in exporting. The opening-up of communications in the nineteenth century – firstly by stage coach and canals, and later by steam railway – accompanied by the increasing mechanisation from industrial development, which greatly altered the shape of the countryside. By 1850 some five thousand miles of railway track were in use which, together with the associated embankments and cuttings, once again disturbed an already segmented landscape. But the development of steam also produced steam ploughing and drainage of land previously unworked.

The first twenty years of the nineteenth century were dominated by the Napoleonic Wars and their aftermath, and one effect was that grain farming, particularly in Britain, became immensely profitable. Trevelyan quotes an example of this: 'The spleen of Cobbett was moved by the number of farmers who at the end of the reign of George III lived in smart new red brick houses – sometimes entitled Waterloo Farm – who drove a gig to market, had wine on the table and a piano in the parlour for their daughters'. This was followed by thirty years of relative hardship as Europe gradually opened up to free trade and grain prices fell, taking food prices down with them. When grain farming became less profitable for land-owners, a shift of emphasis took place on estates towards grassland with associated dairy products, while the development of the sporting potential, often giving increased rents, speeded up tree planting for the growing interest in covert shooting.

It is not always realised that in the middle of the nineteenth century some three-quarters of the countryside was still in the hands of private landowners, while the remaining quarter was held by yeoman farmers, or institutional owners such as the Church, the Crown, and hospitals, colleges and charities who had received land from benefactors. Land conferred political power on its owners: it was a major economic resource in the British Isles, and even in 1850 was the largest single employer of labour. At that time, half the sixteen million population of England and Wales lived and worked in the countryside, employed in farming and the many small rural industries, such as weaving and spinning, which also employed the wives and children of agricultural families. The Great Exhibition of 1851 held in the Crystal Palace, specially erected in London's Hyde Park, accelerated the swing to industrialisation, which favoured concentration in factories. The rush to the towns had begun, and the population of London had reached two million inhabitants. It is said that the glass exhibition hall was plagued by the droppings of sparrows which defied capture. Queen Victoria sent for the aged Duke of Wellington whose advice was prompt and straightforward: 'Try sparrowhawks, madam'.

Then in the middle years of the century as industrialisation became a force in the land, a second rich period in British farming began with the demand for meat, vegetables and dairy produce from the growing urban populations of the new towns. This trend continued until the late 1870s when a succession of bad harvests, together with increasing cheap imports of food, meat and grain from the Americas and Australasia, brought about further radical changes in farming fortunes and methods, favouring the grazing of grasslands in place of corn. But soon two million acres of poorer land lay fallow and unfarmed again, and much of this came to be used in one way or another for hunting and shooting.

Land left uncultivated soon reverts to scrub bushes and undergrowth, which is attractive as food and cover for birds and wild animals, pheasants and partridges included. Worthless for farming, it can be preserved for shooting or hunting. Nesting birds bring in the seeds of trees and before long some small saplings of the local varieties start to appear. Left alone they increase in height and number, with further saplings seeding themselves in the open cover. Eventually a mixed woodland emerges which, with only a little attention, can continue to improve both visually and as a habitat for wildlife. In this way, fox coverts planted initially with gorse can become mixed woodlands after a number of years.

Landed estates and the country house

During these lean periods for arable farming in the nineteenth century there were significant changes in the emphasis of land use. Landowners who derived their income from wider sources than their estates alone – such as coal, minerals and rents in the growing cities – were in a better position to weather the fluctuations of prices over this century (for instance during the farm slump of 1847 corn prices varied between £6 per ton and £2 10s per ton, and many corn dealers and bill brokers were ruined). Such broad-based sources of income permitted the continuity of landed estates in periods of poor agricultural returns. Sir Arthur Bryant wrote:

'An English landed estate in the first half of the nineteenth century was a masterpiece of smooth and intricate organisation . . . farms, gardens, dairies, brewhouses, granaries, stables, laundries and workshops . . . its kitchens, larders and sculleries, beer and wine cellars, gunrooms and stores . . . such houses were the headquarters of what was still the chief industry of England – agriculture.'

The English country house had become the hub of the estate that it controlled and was now the power base of the family who lived in it, providing them also with political prestige if they wished to use it. It was also the centre for a large number of outdoor activities with rooms set aside for guns and fishing rods, tack and harness; game larders, kennels and stables were accommodated in a range of out-buildings. Soon the interiors of country houses were also hung with a variety of sporting paintings alongside those that had been collected by their owners or their ancestors on the Grand Tour. The life of the English squire and his taste for sport had become married to the necessity to maintain good returns from agriculture and forestry, which the increasing sophistication of life in the English country house demanded.

Sporting rather than landed interests took on an increasing value, as the new wealthy professional and industrial urban classes took up hunting

An English country estate with Manor House and architectural embellishment. Early 19th century English school.

Above: Coursing – two gentlemen with a pair of greyhounds. John Nost Sartorius, dated 1806. *Left*: Gentleman with two pointers and gamekeeper. John Nost Sartorius, dated 1814.

and shooting on a big scale both for leisure and for the social opportunities they provided. In the process estates and countryside received a great deal of care and attention, and much more money was spent on the land to the benefit of fox-hunting, and to game birds and their habitat. These are the main sports which have had a visually stimulating effect on the landscape that we see today. Indeed, it is probable that as much of our lovely countryside was created by sporting landowners because of the gun as had earlier been created by the axe or the plough.

Sporting landowners and their estates

Two notable sporting landowners were Lord Townshend and Mr Thomas Coke, later Lord Leicester of Holkham in Norfolk. The former converted thousands of acres of the waterlogged breckland of East Anglia into good arable farming land, which also became good sporting countryside. The first Coke and his successors were the archetypal squires of the developing British agriculture from the 1650s onwards. In their first two hundred years they turned a light, sandy, unproductive soil – pockmarked with rabbit warrens – into a model estate which at one time extended to nearly fifty thousand acres, and was visited by agriculturalists from all over Britain and Europe. Later the second Earl of Leicester assisted the then Prince of Wales in the improvement of Sandringham as a sporting estate.

He and other pioneers had introduced 'marling' to improve the soil fertility; the east Midland marl and clay subsoil stratum was dug up and mixed into the light topsoil to strengthen it. Some of these open marl pits – often dug every fifty acres or so – became ponds and were useful for watering farm stock, sheep and wildfowl. Others throughout the farmlands of the eastern counties developed into wild sanctuaries of shrubs and trees.

With moderate rents on the tenanted farms to discourage exploitation and consequent over-cropping of the soil, the Cokes produced in time an estate which included both arable farming and sheep grazing. Farming and forestry were both practised at Holkham in a way which has given unity to much of the landscape. Many of the woodlands were planted before 1800, and the estate was ringed by a thick belt of trees to lessen the effects of the prevailing winds. Both were mature when pheasant shooting got into its stride. Scarborough Clump is said to be the first place in England where pheasants were actually driven over the guns. Certainly the Cokes of Holkham were among the foremost sportsmen to develop the pheasant as a bird of sport.

More recent trends

Developments on farm lands in Britain continue apace. In the three decades since the end of the Second World War, we have seen higher yields of grain from new varieties of corn, and the introduction of new crops into the rotation, such as oilseed rape and linseed, which add vivid yellows and blues to the landscape. The sophisticated tractor and the combine harvester have ousted the old methods of farming: the reaper and binder, the threshing machine and fields full of stooked corn towards the end of the summer are things of the past.

Above: Setting out for the Moors. Thomas Edge Jnr. on his pony with William Atkinson his Dog Man; the retriever Prince and two pointers Rake and Romp. John Ferneley Snr., dated Melton Mowbray 1842. *Below*: Mr and Mrs Andrews at the time of the harvest of 1750 on their estate near Sudbury, Suffolk. It is said that the artist painted out a brace of partridges originally laid on Mrs Andrews' lap. The detail (*above right*) shows the mixed farming of wheat and sheep, making for good partridge country. Thomas Gainsborough.

IV
Sporting Art
as a Pictorial Archive

Sporting painting in England began at the time of the Tudors and Stuarts, who were devoted to the chase and to horsemanship. In *The Complete Gentleman* (1622) Henry Peacham remarks:

'Hawking and hunting are recreations very commendable and befitting a noble or gentleman to exercise.'

Not many years later François de la Rochefoucauld in *A Frenchman's England* wrote:

'One of the Englishman's greatest joys is in field sports – they are all quite mad about them.'

The Melton Hunt going to draw Rams Head Covert. A major picture with a plate identifying all the personalities. Sir Francis Grant (1803–78), dated 1838.

Stella A. Walker in the introductory paragraphs of *Sporting Art – England 1700–1900* (1972) gives an insight into the subject of sporting art and landscape painting:

'The school of British sporting art is unique. From all the early animal, hawking and hunting pictures by continental artists no traditional treatment of the sporting subject emerged as it did in England, where hunting, racing and the development of the Thoroughbred horse not only encouraged but in fact instigated a national school of sporting art . . .

'It has been said that Walpole invariably opened the letters from his gamekeeper and huntsman before those of his sovereign, and in England this age-old love of sport could be considered a peculiar national trait that was not confined, as on the continent, almost solely to royalty and the court. The Englishman's home was not a castle, but a country house where he could keep horses and hounds, and try to breed them faster and finer than his neighbour.

'Though the aristocracy took precedence, only second in standing was the English country gentleman, for a rural property was the foundation of dignity and respect. Fortunes produced by commerce were astutely invested in country estates. By the nineteenth century every man of standing in Europe had adopted the English riding dress, not to indicate he was a horseman but that he was a *country* gentleman. This essential quality the British sporting artist has recorded for posterity in pictures, which also provide a vivid documentary of the changing face of the English countryside between 1700 and 1900, when agriculture was emerging as the principal industry and sporting customs were being transformed to meet the new conditions.

Left: Death of the stag in Windsor Great Park near the present Royal Lodge. The Prince of Wales is in hunting livery with a party of notables. *Right*: The return from the Chase, showing the Prince of Wales with his party and huntsmen in livery and the east front of Windsor Castle in the background. John Wootton, both dated 1737. Reproduced by gracious permission of Her Majesty the Queen.

'This task required a many-sided talent, for not only were artistic facility and vision necessary, but also detailed knowledge of both human and animal anatomy allied to an understanding of the esoteric intricacies and traditions of field sports. A good likeness was not enough for the dedicated sportsman: every detail of horse and hound, every bit and breastplate, every shotgun and rod, had to be correct. Hardship of travel was also a perennial handicap to the artist; good health and endurance were required for frequent journeys by coach from Newmarket to Scotland, from Melton Mowbray to Yorkshire, in winter storms and summer heat. With these demands and conditions no wonder artistic standards were uneven; it is something of a miracle that these men so often produced pleasing and important pictures of the English country way of life and occasionally, for our delight today, paintings that are minor masterpieces by any artistic criterion.'

At the end of the eighteenth century the countryside was becoming softer and more orderly as wild areas were conquered and cultivated, scrubland cleared, wetlands drained, woodlands planted and much of the old remaining forest brought under control. The sporting landscape painters began to reach new heights of technique throughout the century, as the animals of the earlier painters gave way to more vital beasts which bore a closer relationship to their background. These wonderful pictorial records of sporting art – both paintings and the widely produced engravings, prints and mezzotints – illustrate more than anything else the beauty of our sporting landscape and the many changes of its development.

The large number of such pictures, so coveted throughout the world, attests to the myriad views which the British Isles have encompassed in their history. They include the delightful sporting conversation pieces of families and their animals painted by Francis Hayman, Arthur Devis and Sir Joshua Reynolds, as well as Gainsborough's early masterpiece, Mr and Mrs Robert Andrews in their Suffolk estate at the time of the harvest of 1750; the very essence of pride in the countryside and its sport. Whereas Reynolds and Devis were essentially townsmen, both Gainsborough and Constable were countrymen born and bred, and, whilst Gainsborough painted portraits for his income, his real love was in painting the countryside.

Only in the last fifty years or so has a school of British sporting art become fully recognised in its own right. Earlier it had been included within a generalisation of landscape or animal paintings. By bringing together in this book the many influences of rural sports on the landscape there emerges coincidentally many of the various underlying aspects of what our sporting art is all about. These British paintings are an important record of our rural way of life, but also, since they contain animals, humans and movement as well as landscape, they are of vital artistic significance. However, many lesser known but highly important painters often have been ignored. John Wootton (1677?–1765), Sawrey Gilpin (1733–1807), James Ward (1769–1859) and the artists of the nineteenth century merit places as portrayers of the social scene in England by their paintings which span nearly two hundred years.

Left: Hare hunting in the open landscape. James Seymour.

Below: The Grosvenor Hunt, 1762. The climax of a deer hunt in the grounds of Eaton Hall, Cheshire. Lord Grosvenor is mounted on Honest John by the tree. George Stubbs.

Birds and decoy at Clandon Park,
Surrey. Francis Barlow.

Two gentlemen preparing for
shooting, with a view of Cresswell
Crags, Derbyshire, or 'Shooting I'.
George Stubbs, dated 1769.

The earliest Primitive sporting art, dating from the Tudor and Stuart period, embraces paintings of houses set in deer parks and frequently pictures of great horses, usually lifesize, as embellishments to the decoration of the larger manor houses. The early hunting scenes generally portrayed royalty and the nobility, but they were often more stage sets for the elaborate court hunting dress of the time. The few romanticised hunting scenes of the seventeenth century tended to draw upon Flemish and French influences, a style which persisted into later periods in some artists' work.

Undoubtedly the father of British sporting art was Francis Barlow (1626–1704), who is the link between traditional English painting, continental art and the hunting tapestries of the earlier period. He was one of the first English artists to specialise in painting birds, animals and sporting subjects, generally in an actual landscape. He was also an engraver, and produced many prints to illustrate early books.

John Wootton, who painted until 1764, emerges as one of the most skilled of early English artists, producing a wide range of sporting, military and landscape scenes. Most of these were large pictures assigned to fit panels in the new internal decorations of country seats such as Badminton, Longleat and Althorp. He possessed great ability to compose large groups of figures and animals in panoramic landscapes; many depicted hunting, hawking and shooting scenes.

As the interest in horseracing increased throughout the countryside it became fashionable to commission paintings of famous horses and racing events. Some of the paintings of Newmarket from the early 1700s onwards fall into the primitive period, but unfortunately many were allowed to decay beyond repair on the walls of hunting boxes, in attics or even in outhouses. The representation of the horse remained somewhat wooden and stilted throughout this time, and early artists had considerable difficulty in portraying their movements. The paintings of James Seymour (1702–52) and Francis Sartorius (1735–1804) particularly illustrate what has come to be called the 'rocking-horse' era. They produced superb compositions of animals in landscape but never quite captured their actions across the ground when galloping. It was a problem with which most sporting artists had to wrestle. Both men painted important studies of hare hunting, and Sartorius also spanned the years of change from the hare to the fox. It was not until the later part of the nineteenth century, when early photographs arrested the true action of galloping, that artists started to portray real movement in racing and hunting pictures. Nevertheless these early paintings have considerable charm and an abundance of interest. Much of the detail is in itself of historical significance as it is so often correct: harness, apparel, guns, dogs and the style and fashion of the time.

The 1760s saw a renaissance of our sporting art. Most of the preceding generation of painters had passed on, and with them their primitive style. There was a new feeling for atmosphere. Now the animals became better related to their surroundings. Stubbs and Gilpin led the new generation to produce a number of masterpieces and many skilled works of considerable artistic merit.

George Stubbs (1724–1806), who was to have such a great influence on later sporting artists, became so obsessed with the study of anatomy in his early years that he was commissioned to illustrate various medical

Jason, beating Brilliant, the Great Subscription Match.

Nathaniel Curzon's 'Jason' beating W. Croft's 'Brilliant' in the Great Subscription Purse at Newmarket in 1754. A match between owners to determine the value of their breeding lines. Francis Sartorius.

tomes with his own engravings. He was afterwards to spend eighteen months dissecting horses layer by layer in a Lincolnshire barn, producing the *Anatomy of the Horse* in 1766. Leonardo da Vinci had carried out similar work on human cadavers in Florence two hundred years earlier, enabling him to make the transformation from the wooden Madonna-like figures of early times to the realism found in his own and later artists' works of the Italian Renaissance. A contemporary of Stubbs, Richard Wilson, is generally looked on as the father of English landscape painting. It is likely that they would have met in Rome in 1754 as their visits would have just overlapped, and then again in London where each worked and exhibited. Between 1759 and 1762 Stubbs produced some of his most elaborate sporting landscapes, combining his talents both for painting horses and men, and for portraying them in the heart of real English countryside. The Goodwood hunting and shooting scenes, as well as those of the Grosvenor Hunt, rank among his finest works. His four large shooting pictures (now in the Yale Center for British Art) were painted between 1768 and 1770: these masterpieces were also engraved by Woollett, who produced prints from these studies.

Sawrey Gilpin (1733–1807), a prolific painter of horses in a lifelike style, often collaborated with landscape artists such as George Barret and William Marlow to achieve composite pictures. George Garrard (1760–1826), James Ward (1769–1859), Ben Marshall (1767–1835) and John Nost Sartorius (1759–1824) were significant painters of the generation following Stubbs. They developed the theme of sporting art for its own sake in a wider context and with less formality.

Soon the way was opened for a Popular era of sporting art, which embraced a broad range of paintings relating to shooting, angling, hunting, coaching, racing, country pastimes and a variety of sporting animals. This period lasted until the middle of the nineteenth century. Speed and travel were portrayed in pictures of hunting and coaching with their attendant spills and accidents. Among the wide variety of artists at this time John Ferneley, James Pollard and John Herring were predominant, with others such as Abraham Cooper and Richard Ansdell. Sporting prints, often of hunting scenes, began to grow in demand and were made available in fairly large quantities. Many were in a lighter vein of caricature and played a considerable part in increasing the enjoyment of sporting art throughout the countryside. Some, like the numerous sets produced by Henry Alken Snr., were engraved directly, with only minor alterations, from original oil paintings: other sets of prints were made from a wide variety of such sporting scenes set in an appropriate landscape.

Well-known flat-racing horses, steeplechasers and hunters continued to have their portraits painted by artists like John Ferneley, but Herring's racing pictures are perhaps the most important in portraying the detail of events and the courses. Shooting pictures, both paintings and prints, were made by many artists of the Popular era. Henry Alken Snr. and Dean Wolstenholme Snr. were among the more prolific painters but Samuel Howitt (1765–1822) should be mentioned for his twenty watercolours for Orme's Collection of *British Field Sports*. Many artists, including some landscape painters like Julius Caesar Ibbetson (1759–1817) produced a variety of shooting themes. Most of these shooting pictures show small numbers of sportsmen with guns, two or three dogs, perhaps a keeper or

Left: Greyhounds and a terrier. George Garrard. *Right*: Mr W. B. Wilson's grey hunter and a Newfoundland shooting dog – almost identical to today's Labrador. John Ferneley Snr., dated 1837.

dog-handler and a pack horse. They are set in country suitable for the quarry: farmlands for partridge and open woodlands for woodcock and pheasant. Similarly pictures of angling in varied settings were produced as the techniques of the sport developed. While some lovely landscape compositions were the work of artists outside a school of sporting art such as

Coursing at Stonehenge. S. Spode, dated 1845.

The finish of the 1833 Goodwood Cup. Mr Kent's 'Rubini' beating Mr Greville's 'Whale' and Lord Exeter's 'Beiram'. James Pollard.

SHOOTING.

J.M.W. Turner and John Constable – who both used figures fishing as a focal point – many angling paintings have come to us from sporting artists such as Abraham Cooper (himself a fisherman), James Pollard and, though he also painted both shooting and hunting, Philip Reinagle (1749–1833). Also the catch was shown lying on the bank, with a house in the distance, by Stephen Elmer (d1796) and by A.E. Rolfe (c1815–88).

Significant events, painted on large canvases to fill the great Victorian houses, became more popular. These embraced crowded racing scenes and big coursing meetings such as Ansdell's Waterloo Cup of 1840; even the large agricultural shows which were becoming established. The scope widened to include pictures of village fairs, sheep shearings, prize cattle and ploughing matches. Some excellent portraits of sporting groups in the countryside were painted for many years, like the conversation pieces of earlier times.

Sporting paintings of the early Victorian era often show varieties of the curly rough-coated Newfoundland fisherman's dog being used for shooting, certainly by 1835. There is however an 1803 print by Richard Earlom (1743–1822) which shows a Newfoundland retrieving a young child from a stream. This larger, strong and long-haired type had probably been bred to swim out with the netlines, while the lighter, smoother-coated strain was established during the century and was used as a shooting dog to retrieve wildfowl and, sometimes, fish falling from the nets in shore waters.

An era of broadly-based Victorian romantic painting followed the popular period and is exemplified by the work of Sir Edwin Landseer (1802–73). Artists depicted animals in romanticised settings as they looked

for new methods of portraying the countryside. Most rural landscapes now also took on a contrived aura of well-being, as their quiteness was interrupted by the coming of the railways, dividing almost symbolically the old world values from the industrial revolution. Highland scenes were in vogue as people travelled to the wilder landscapes of Scotland, though these are mostly outside the range of sporting art.

The Modern period of horse painting was dominated by Sir Alfred Munnings (1878–1959), who continued the earlier traditions, working for nearly sixty years from the turn of the century. Here the style of his work is lighter and less photographic and seems sometimes influenced by a kind of impressionism. Munnings was a painter from an unusual mould. He sold his early paintings to buy hunters and later in life bought racehorses which he used as models. He also painted open landscapes which have a tranquil peace contrasting sharply with the pent-up excitement which he captured at the start of a race and with the whole atmosphere of the racecourse. His brood mares under stately trees in the English countryside may be compared with studies by Gilpin and Stubbs. Lionel Edwards (1878–1966) also painted many sporting pictures with traditional realism and a sensitive understanding of English country life.

From the end of the nineteenth century birds were more often painted. Many pictures stemmed from the technical accuracy of the great sporting naturalist, John Millais (1865–1931) in his *Game Birds and Shooting Sketches* (1892) and from Charles Whymper's studies in Charles Dixon's *The Game Birds and Wild Fowl of the British Isles* (1893): two of the finest books on British birds. Thorburn, Lodge and Tunnicliffe followed these with accurately portrayed bird studies in woodland, moorland and waterside settings.

Islands such as ours have an ever-changing panorama of skyscape, particularly near the coasts, while inland the cloud shadows give an infinite

variety to the colour values of the landscape. In the 1930s and 40s Sir Peter Scott, and later Hugh Monahan, started a long series of estuary and river pictures of wildfowl carefully shown in flight, often against a vivid skyscape.

In 1960 a most memorable exhibition of fifty-three paintings was held at the Virginia Museum in Richmond, U.S.A., entitled *Sport and the Horse*. This was followed by other similar exhibitions, which culminated in the brilliant and eye-opening *British Sporting Paintings 1650–1850*, covering also such diverse activities as angling, cricket and even rat-catching. It was held in 1974 at the Hayward Gallery in London under the auspices of the Arts Council of Great Britain. The breadth of the exhibition and its effect on the art world were gratifying, but unless it is followed by the establishment of an appropriate gallery to show these fascinating paintings, future generations may be denied what could be considered the most enlightened of

Huntsman and hounds at a covert. Sam Alken.

70

The Raby Hunt, Yorkshire. John Nost
Sartorius.

all English art. Fortunately there is now a growing awareness of the heritage
of sporting art in Britain and, as a great step forward, in 1977 the British
Sporting Art Trust was formed to establish a permanent collection for a
special gallery at the Tate and also for another centre in the north of
England at York.

It is hoped that notable pictures from the many private collections
will eventually find their way into the new national archive rather than be
dispersed to the four corners of the world as a result of taxation, distribution
or the death of the original owner. Outside the magnificent collections at
the residences of Her Majesty The Queen, the largest single accumulation
of eighteenth and nineteenth century sporting art today is at the Yale
Center for British Art set up by the Mellon Foundation at Newhaven,
Connecticut, U.S.A. which is housed in a modern gallery built and lit
specifically for viewing and study.

A large early Newfoundland fishing dog retrieving a ring-necked cock pheasant. Philip Reinagle, c1795.

A catch of fish on the bank of a stream – brown trout, roach and carp. Stephen Elmer, of Farnham, c1775.

Right: Dead game, a study of blackcock, pheasants, grey partridges and a brown hare. Edward Coleman, dated 1825.

Over page
Left: The outer kitchen hung with game and vegetables, with the keeper's spaniel and pointer, perhaps waiting to be fed. Edmund Bristow, dated 1831.
Right: The saddling enclosure at Cheltenham Races. Sir Alfred Munnings.
Blackcock, greyhen and red grouse on the lochside; from *British Birds* (1914). Archibald Thorburn.
Flighting Pink Feet on the Solway. Hugh Monahan, dated 1949.

Speed – the Cambridgeshire Hunt in full
cry. J. F. Herring Snr., dated 1845.

V
Rural Sports and the Landscape

Speed – the factor in the Chase from the 18th century

The many rural sports which have been enjoyed throughout Britain for centuries have not, except for the earlier deer hunting, made the visual impact on the landscape of fox-hunting and game shooting as practised after the Restoration and particularly from the eighteenth century onwards. The partridge, the pheasant, the deer, the fox and the horse were in their various ways responsible for substantial changes in our countryside. Increased speed in horseracing was to affect fox-hunting, while new skills in the faster driven partridge shooting gave rise to the *battues* of Victorian times.

Shooting Flying. From *The Gentleman's Recreation.*

Shooting flying – the supreme challenge

The popularity of hawking was at its height at the end of the fourteenth century, but before the end of the seventeenth it was waning, to give way to shooting. Relatively little about the sport has come down to us in picture form, unlike the shooting and hunting of later centuries. Hawking did continue, but was now often surrounded by more ceremonial. It was revived for a time by Colonel Thomas Thornton (c1755–1823) who also went on sporting tours with a large entourage and accompanied by hawks, game guns, rifles and dogs of different kinds. On his famous tour of Scotland in 1784 he also took with him the artist George Garrard. Born to enormous wealth Thornton was an enthusiast for nearly every kind of country sport. Later as enclosures and ploughland took over the waste areas he sought a new home in Wiltshire so that he could fly the hawks he loved on the open downlands.

The predominant game birds of the countryside were to become the partridge and the pheasant, with snipe and wildfowl in the marshes and estuaries. But in these earlier times a much greater variety of 'game' birds was hunted: green and golden plover, bittern, curlew, landrail, fieldfare, pigeon and of course woodcock – at one time more plentiful in the woodlands than pheasant. However, people did not plant coverts for visiting or migratory birds and as their numbers declined many were placed on a protected list to assist them to maintain their numbers.

One delightful piece of nonsense which illustrates the kind of advice given about the problems of the new art of shooting flying was included in Richard Blome's *The Gentleman's Recreation*:

'Some are of the opinion that you must shoot something before the fowl, otherwise it will be passed before the shot can come to it, but that is a vulgar error: for no Game can fly so quick, but that the shot will meet it.'

This obviously refers to the amount of forward lead to be given; a matter which still occupies the pages of the shooting periodicals, as it means different things to different people. Shooting flying meant shooting more accurately and faster as sporting guns were improved. Speed now entered sport and many of the old quieter activities were soon influenced by the change.

Above: Partridge shooting in a tidy landscape. *Right*: Horse racing. Both prints by Samuel Howitt from Orme's *Collection of British Field Sports*, published in 1807.

Racing gets well established

The racecourse was the supreme test of a horse's speed, stamina and soundness, and it was the only reliable guide to the selection of breeding stock and the establishment of blood lines. With this went the careful compilation of stud books. Early racing, often between just two or three horses, was a competition with wagers between owners to test their bloodstock. Because of continued royal patronage, horse races were firmly popular with the nobility and the gentry, many of whom maintained private studs. Officers of the military also became greatly interested in improving

the horse, as the proven stallions could now cover good country-bred mares. Such was the search for fine Arab stallions that the Darley Arabian is said to have been found in Syria at the turn of the seventeenth century by a younger son obliged to seek his fortune.

After the Restoration of the Monarchy racing was immediately commenced in earnest and important courses with stands, rails and good turf were developed at Bath, York and Epsom Downs. Many Newmarket races at this time consisted of four one mile heats and a final course to develop the breeding of good stout horses; the need to rub down the horses in between led to the 'rubbing house' seen in so many early paintings of racecourses. The Rowley mile at Newmarket was named after a famous stallion of the day, Old Rowley, used by King Charles II as his hack.

Queen Anne favoured racing at Ascot Heath, just outside Windsor Great Park, where the gently rising ground and sandy gravel subsoil provided an ideal setting. The conditions were suited to the faster racing resulting from the developments of thoroughbred blood lines. This course superseded the old low-lying royal course used in Charles II's time beside the Thames and below the castle at Datchet Ferry, which was later to be used for horse shows.

The thoroughbred racehorse was established by the beginning of the eighteenth century in the form which has come down to the present day. Soon races and rules proliferated as local bodies promoted their own events, and fields became larger. The near chaos that ensued as outside betting money was attracted could not be allowed to continue. By 1752 the Jockey Club was set up by noble and gentlemen owners at Newmarket to rule over all aspects of British racing. Under local control, but qualified by Jockey Club rules, many different races were devised. Sweepstakes with larger fields became popular. Races were shorter and faster, with more of them at each meeting, but it was not until after the Ascot meeting of 1791 that handicaps became a feature.

To meet the need of a growing London population, much of it of country stock, an attempt was made to introduce race meetings and a training area within the Metropolis. A large portion of land was acquired near Notting Hill, where stabling and boxes for about seventy-five horses were erected with every convenience for a training establishment. A good racecourse was formed, and numerous stakes were run on it in 1838. But the promoters overlooked one important aspect, at once fatal to the Hippodrome: the soil was a deep strong clay, so that the training ground could only be used in some weathers. This could not be overcome and the racecourse closed its short career. It was at about this time that the London to Newmarket road was considerably improved and straightened to cut down the travelling time to the course, which now became the undisputed

A sweepstake for 200 guineas on the Beacon course, Newmarket, in September 1767. Mr Shafton's 'Ferdinando' (8st 0lbs) beating Mr Meynell's 'Spry' (8st 6lbs). Francis Sartorius.

'The Chances of the Steeplechase'. James Pollard.

centre of racing. Driving their phaetons, the sports cars of the nineteenth century, gentlemen could reach out a hundred miles from London for a long weekend.

The first recorded steeplechase was in Ireland in 1752 when two hunting squires, Blake and O'Callaghan, challenged one another to ride four and a half miles across country from Buttevant church steeple to St Mary's steeple, Doneraile. The first 'chase to be recorded in England was between some officers of the Life Guards at Nacton near Ipswich in 1803, riding out from barracks in the full moon with their uniforms covered by their nightshirts. A steeplechase for a sweepstake of twenty-five sovereigns for the winner across open country over a 'marked' course (indicated by flags at key points) was organised about 1831 for officers of the Life Guards by Tommy Coleman, a well-known trainer and the owner of the Chequers Inn, later the Turf Hotel at St Albans. He laid out a course which started and finished near his inn to enable him to judge the result. Fifteen horses raced from the hill where Harlington church stands and then over four miles of fast hunting country to the obelisk in Wrest Park. By 1832 the meeting was a public one, and on March 8th twenty riders came to the

Above: A named field in the St Albans Grand Steeple Chase, March 8th 1832 – probably the first public steeplechase for sweepstakes. *Left*: The Cheltenham Annual Grand Steeple Chase, 1841.

The Cheltenham Grand Annual Steeplechase, April 18th 1862. Claude Lorraine
Ferneley.

line including Captain Becher, after whom the Grand National brook was
named. Usually the last horse home had to pay the stake of the second
horse, which often helped to produce some fine rear finishes. The scenes
were painted by J. Pollard and a set of engravings was made. The St
Albans meeting lasted for a few years only, as it attracted large and
unmanageable crowds and was soon opposed both by moralists and by
agricultural factions because of the damage inflicted on the farmland. The
last St Albans race was run in 1838.

A set of engraved prints by F. C. Turner, dated 1839, shows the first
Liverpool Grand National Steeplechase being run over a closed course with
jumps and brick-built stands at Aintree; translating the glory that had been
St Albans'. The new course, which became the centre of steeplechasing,
was then owned by the famous Mr Lynn of the Waterloo Hotel at Aintree.
He also established the Waterloo Cup in 1836 for the coursing champion-
ship held nearby at Altcar.

It was not until the National Hunt Committee drew up rules in 1866
for what came to be called point-to-point races (those ridden in a direct
line from one marked obstacle by way of various others to a finishing place
for prize money) that these events developed to become one of the financial
props of fox-hunting. Now they are held over open country courses with
specially constructed hedge and ditch jumps.

The Hare – a link between the stag and modern fox-hunting

The brown hare is a beast of venery and has been hunted by scent since early times, both on foot and on horseback with the slow southern hounds and then with harriers. It has also been coursed by greyhounds, hunted by the larger hawks, stalked with crossbows and, more recently, shot with rifle and shotgun. Hares have been a source of fresh meat through the winter months for countless generations of country folk, as well as providing sport through the centuries for young and old, squire and artisan. The hare can claim a unique place in our rural sports as the only animal to have been hunted, hawked and shot regularly for a thousand years, while until very recently maintaining· a reasonably constant population level in Britain, though not across the Channel. Its only respite came from its protection from shooting in James I's Act of *c*1614, which was repealed in 1807 and was designed to preserve the animal for hunting.

Hares are indigenous to the British Isles, and of the two main species, the brown hare inhabits nearly all low open terrains from plains to downland and most open woodlands where it can shelter. The highest hare populations exist in the eastern counties and generally in chalk and limestone country. The blue or mountain hare is confined to the higher moor or mountainous ground of Snowdonia, the Lake District and Scotland. It also populates Ireland where the brown hare is absent.

When the forest laws concerning deer were imposed by the Normans, the hunting of the hare was the sport of ordinary people in the country. In many parts of the land as the forest deer retreated and park deer began to be preserved for the Chase, the hare, always a wild creature composed for speed, was more and more valued for sport, both in open woodlands and in fields. Its habit of running in circles round its home ground made hunting it popular with the young who liked the Chase and the elderly who

'Finding the Hare', a print after Dean Wolstenholme.

could watch hound-work by taking short cuts. Edward Plantagenet, 2nd Duke of York, in his treatise on hunting, *The Master of Game* written between 1406 and 1413 to instruct Henry V in the art of hunting, placed the hare above deer in order of precedence of the Chase.

'It is to be known that the hare is king of all venery; for blowing and the fair terms of hunting cometh of the seeking and finding of the hare. For certain it is the most marvellous beast that is.'

The period of the Civil War did great damage to the game animals of Britain, with bands of hungry soldiers and vagabonds roaming the forests, removing estate fencing for fuel and poaching parks for deer. The days of the sacrosanct Norman royal deer were gone for ever, but the hare population soon recovered. It was an easy and gradual transformation to develop hounds for hunting the hare instead of the wild deer, and it soon became very popular. The countryside had become progressively denuded of woodlands as demands for timber increased, so that by the Restoration of 1660 there were many open tracts of country which had previously been the habitat of the wild deer. Many of these now became suitable for hare hunting.

In most English counties there was a long interval between the steady retreat of the deer to more desolate and uncultivated districts and the commencement of organised fox-hunting, which would eventually become 'modern fox-hunting'. It spanned two centuries in some areas, and during this period the hare was supreme as the most noble beast of the chase in open country. Hunting generally started in the middle of September and ended in February so as not to destroy the leverets. The sport was carried out in the early morning when the scent was fresh and the hares most likely

Brown hare in her form. Rodger McPhail.

Opposite
Top and below right: two of a set of four
coursing scenes – 'In View' and 'Slipping'.
Sam Alken. *Below left*: Hare hunting – a
print by Samuel Howitt.

to be found on their forms: it combined the country arts of understanding weather, ground and scent, all of which signs had to be carefully interpreted for a successful chase. Hares were held to know the changes in the weather from one day to another, and when hunted regularly were fast and very intelligent in their use of terrain, often taking to the country highways in bad conditions. Harrier packs were specifically bred for particular country and 'entered' to the hare so as to learn its scent: they were not used for deer, fox or otter hunting. It was hard in those days to breed an even kennel of fast hounds that were of equal speed and packed well.

Some hound packs in the first half of the eighteenth century hunted the scent of whichever quarry they found, be it hare or fox. Most were dedicated to the hare, still considered noble as in France, but occasionally people who had found and hunted the fox and enjoyed it turned away from the hare or the deer. One such was the Fifth Duke of Beaufort who in 1762, when still a minor, returning after a poor morning's stag-hunting, found a fast late morning fox in Silk Wood. He gave such a good run into open country that the Badminton hounds were thereafter encouraged to the fox.

Another field sport which gained in popularity in the eighteenth century was the coursing of hares, and here again speed played a large part. The Swaffham Coursing Society was founded in Norfolk in 1776 by Lord Orford, who is said to have crossed the greyhound of his day with the bulldog, and persevered with the experiment to the sixth or seventh generation. Czarina was one of Lord Orford's breed and she ran forty-seven courses without defeat.

It is surprising that our hare is held in such lowly recognition in Britain today when the richness of its contribution to sporting activities has been so broadly based. Hares appear infrequently in sporting art, except when hunted on horseback in early times, as in the delightful canvases of James Seymour (1702–52), and only incidentally in landscapes, when in fact the countryside has been full of them for centuries. Perhaps because hunters tend to respect each other's quarry, the hare – abandoned by the fox-hunter as ground game – never attracted the game shot who was already dedicated to shooting flying by the time its protection from shooting was repealed. Certainly in some farming areas hares are abundant enough to be pests and are awarded the same status as the crop-destroying rabbit. In grazing land it is said that ten hares can eat as much grass as one sheep. The winter hare-drives, in which the tenant farmers, gamekeepers, pickers-up, village constabulary and others often join, are to the shoot owner more of an exercise in pest control than a quest for challenging shooting. Any feelings of *noblesse* are now absent.

British sportsmen no longer accord the hare the same reverence or interest as their *confrères* across the Channel. Before the arrival of cold winter days, many an Englishman now discreetly turns the other way when 'puss' lollops out of a covert or slips through a hedge, whereas our continental neighbours often select a hare in preference to a high pheasant. To them it is truly a noble beast, bestowing upon the hunter the same sort of *cachet* as a woodcock. The sight of a hare sends the blood racing through the veins of a Latin or a central European in the same way that the fleeting glimpse of a huge trout, a magnificent stag, or the sound of wild geese passing through the night sky excites our own countrymen.

When fox-hunting started, gentlemen would meet together in the early morning when scenting was good. But a kill 'above ground' was seldom achieved as hounds were then generally slow: the practice was to hunt the 'drag' of the fox back to his earth where he had returned, full of food from his own night's hunting. When it was realised that the mid-morning fox would often run fast and straight across the country it soon lost its vermin label for that of a cunning adversary. The new vogue of fox-hunting above ground is well described in the preface by E. D. Cuming to the 1928 reprint of Nicholas Cox's volume on Hunting of the *Gentleman's Recreation*.

'. . . The earths were stopped and the hounds hunted him in covert . . . "When forced away the fox will lead from wood to wood, a ring of four, six or ten miles and sometimes endways about twenty miles, trying all the earths he knows". Doubtless the change came about slowly as it seems certain that the new method was first adopted in the Northern counties where, says Blome, many preferred hunting a fox because their fast Northern Beagles or "Gazehounds" ran down a hare too quickly; also because a fox-hunt gave their horses more exercise.'

It seems that fox-hunting had become accepted as a sport superior to hare-hunting by 1730. When Sir Robert Walpole wrote to the Earl of Carlisle offering him the Mastership of the Royal Harriers, he pointed out that on the old establishment there had been both a Master of Buckhounds and a Master of Harriers: '. . . but as the Master of Harriers is an ancient and known office, thinks it might be better if . . . the office be called Master of Foxhounds and Harriers'.

Much of the countryside was often inaccessible or too fragmented for the thrills of fox-hunting. Open tracts of grassland were needed, together with larger and better balanced packs of *fast* hounds than had previously been assembled: then came a dedicated group of well-mounted hunting landowners, and finally a wealthy Master whose generalship could bring all together. However, this did not happen overnight; it required the combination of these several components. New methods had to be devised for drawing coverts, and a variety of other skills developed to hunt the new fast quarry.

The dull, undulating grassland of Leicestershire provided the first requirement. Being heavy clay and difficult to farm for corn, much of it was maintained for grazing stock by the large landowners. Because of the number of sizeable estates in this area, open tracts of land were drained and hedged with quickthorn to enclose very much larger fields than were normal in the arable lands.

Hugo Meynell, who took over Quorndon Hall in 1752, provided the leadership to bring together the various factions within that countryside, from the graziers to the landed nobility. He was also knowledgeable enough to learn his blood lines, and the science of line-breeding and out-crossing to produce an even pack of faster foxhounds, marked above all else by drive. Horse breeding by private landowners over the previous century had also started to bring about the part-thoroughbred blood hunter, enabling the 'keen' sporting hunt member to keep right up with the faster hounds.

In Full Chace. ACTION de Chasser.
Inscribed to his Grace CHARLES Duke of Grafton,

Early fox-hunting in the Duke of Grafton's country – 'In Full Chace'. A print dated May 1st 1754 from a painting by James Seymour.

A major factor in Meynell's success was his ability to produce large even packs, not only with a good turn of speed, but with noses to match. By taking the best of the lighter northern hounds which he had inherited and crossing them with a selection of the southern breed for nose, then following a path of rigorous selection, he developed the prototypes of the modern foxhound. A pack of over a hundred couples was now necessary, with hunting on several days in a week. Hound puppies were 'walked' by wives and families of farmers, landowners and hunt followers before going back to kennels for training. Many masters exchanged hounds regularly with other packs to breed out their inconsistencies, among them Peter Beckford who was famous for his breeding of hounds.

Now it was possible to hunt a quicker mid-morning fox which did not generally go to ground, and modern fox-hunting came to be developed in the open Melton Mowbray country, which by 1785 had become almost

Left above: The Charborough Hounds, Dorset, *c*1833. Formed by Mr J. S. W. S. Erle-Drax, their uniform was a yellow coat with a blue collar, generally with grey horses. R. B. Davis (1782–1854). *Left, below*: Fox Hunting. An Ackermann print of the Belvoir country – open landscape dotted with spinneys. *Above*: The meet of Sir Tatton Sykes' hounds at Glebe Farm Grunstone, Leicestershire, showing Birdsdall Clump and Church. John Ferneley Snr., *c*1840.

entirely open grazing land with scattered thorn hedges. A large thrusting pack of the fast lighter hounds would draw coverts towards the middle of the morning, driving the fox into open ground where it was followed by the whole field. The hunt once joined, they hoped, would be kept entirely in the open country, ending in a kill above ground, if the previous night's earthstopping had been well carried out.

The countryside of the Quorn and the Belvoir, the Vales of Aylesbury and the Oxfordshire Windrush might have been sculptured with fox-hunting in mind, providing clear, fast runs in large grass fields separated by challenging hedgerows and with good cover in the many patches of woodland scrub, gorse and spinney. In turn the chase aided the continued development of the hunter and then the steeplechaser as keeping up with the field became a prerequisite for well-heeled enthusiastic followers. The many later prints, depicting the falls and mishaps of the hunting field, illustrate the results of the new taste for speed.

The great contribution which fox-hunting made to the countryside was in the attention brought to the landscape, particularly in the form of financial aid. Hedges were kept in good order, gates and fences properly looked after and marginal grass gallops maintained in open land. Many existing rides were widened or opened up through old dense woodland to the benefit of all wildlife. Enlightened masters improved their coverts to

The Woodland Harriers on the Essex/Suffolk borders, October 25th 1862. Thomas Smythe.

Crossing a brook in the flat, wide open grasslands of the Shires. J. Dalby (c1815–c1860).

The Hertfordshire Hunt. James Pollard,
dated 1839.

increase the number of foxes rather than resorting to 'bagmen' – Leadenhall
Market in the City of London specialised for a time in importing foxes from
Europe for bagmen to sell to masters who had none. All across the country
new woods and copses were planted and coverts improved, especially by
the use of gorse to make them warmer and keep people away.

Social historians have repeatedly asserted that fox-hunting kept a
landed aristocracy anchored to the country estates by making life pleasant
for a leisured class. Horse racing and breeding, point-to-points, fishing,
shooting and hunting all contributed to this attachment to the husbandry
of the countryside and to the vigorous independence of the English squire.
In Europe where a slavish urban court society predominated, the opposite
was often true. This may well have been a factor which accounted for the
horrors of revolt and the burnt-down *châteaux* of absentee nobility. Moreover, since the fox had always been considered vermin, the local populace
could hunt over land by permission of its owners, while the Game Laws
confined the right to hunt or shoot game to landowners with an income of

Full cry towards the regular patchwork fields of enclosure with the promise of many jumps to come. J. F. Herring Snr. (1795–1865).

£100 per year, excepting squires and their eldest sons, but not ordinary countryfolk, even by invitation. The sale of game was also closely controlled to prevent dealing in poached birds. These statutes, enacted in 1671, and echoing those of Norman times, were not repealed until 1831. Cobbett, in his *Rural Rides* of 1820, recorded that as many as a third of all prisoners in local gaols were there because of the Game Laws.

Fox-hunting was a sport developed by time and opportunity. It fulfilled that admirable earlier citing of Eusebius in *The Complete Gentleman* by Henry Peacham on 'Exercise of the Body':

'Wild beasts were of purpose created by God that men by chasing and encountering them might be fitted and enabled for warlike exercises.'

Britain had been spasmodically engaged in a 'hundred years of skirmishes' in Europe following the Treaty of Utrecht in 1713, and mobile cavalry were well established. It is said that it was the habit of mounted officers of riding in their red top-coats when out hunting which led to the adoption of scarlet by most masters in the hunting field. Until then it had been the 'ducal green' for the nobility and drab for the hunt servants. The Duke of Beaufort's livery is still green and the Vale of Aylesbury's yellow was taken from the Old Berkeley Hunt. At the end of the Napoleonic Wars the Duke of Wellington's officers returned to continue their cavalry charges across the grassland shires of England, and a larger second generation of Masters of Foxhounds emerged in the style of Meynell and Beckford. Mytton, Osbaldeston and Assheton-Smith were among them; all possessed great physique.

Top: The Belvoir crossing the Smite. John Ferneley Snr., dated 1830. *Above*: The Vale of Belvoir with Clawson Windmill in the distance. John Ferneley Snr.

In the earlier paintings of fox-hunting, when the season started in the late summer, the settings are often picturesque wooded landscapes, still in leaf. By the reign of George III hunting was forbidden until after harvest, and soon, with the advent of modern fox-hunting, it did not begin seriously until the fall of the leaf.

Fox-hunting provided an almost unlimited opportunity to the artists of the generation after Stubbs – open country, action, horses, hounds and huntsmen in scarlet coats were placed on canvas for posterity. Similarly the landscape, particularly in the Shires, received benefits of which many

Hunting in pewey-type fields. J. F. Herring Snr., dated 1834.

examples remain today. The scattered copses, planted as refuges for foxes, were given names which were defined on the smaller scale maps, and in many cases are still in existence.

Thorpe Trussels in the Quorn country was named from the nearby village of Thorpe and the Saxon word trussels meaning 'a small pocket or parcel of waste land'. The soil was so poor for farming that it was rented to the Hunt and planted as a fox covert. Botany Bay was so called because it was the most distant from the Quorn kennels. It was a large tanglewood area of dense woodland in which it was possible to get hopelessly lost when hunting late; thus it was nick-named after the far-off penal settlement on the east coast of Australia. It does, however, have one of Leicestershire's most prominent landmarks close to it – the Billesdon Coplow peak of nearly six hundred feet – from which one can navigate a route home in the dusk. In 1800, the last year of Meynell's mastership, the Quorn had perhaps the most famous day's hunting of all. A fox led a field starting with two hundred horses some twenty-eight miles to Billesdon Coplow and then evaded them.

The first half of the nineteenth century has been described as the golden age of fox-hunting, with thoroughbred hunters and line-bred foxhounds. It was by now a national sport, no longer a private pursuit enjoyed mainly by the aristocracy and the squires. This was an era of legendary masters and huntsmen, with hunts financed by subscription and supported by increasing numbers of both the rural and the wealthy urban middle class. The coming of the railways, decried across the country because of the demise of the stage coach, in fact made hunting accessible to far more people. Sportsmen now regularly made longer journeys to hunt in the Shires – Leicestershire, Northamptonshire and Rutland – where the best sport was to be found. By 1840 many main railway lines had been built, and it was often easier to box the horses some thirty miles down the line with the groom, rather than hack across country changing horses with a light groom sent on ahead and then hack back in the dusk or on the next day. Tradesmen now hunted alongside the dukes and the landed gentry, and the country benefited from this broader-based relationship, particularly in times of rural tension. Surtees immortalised in *Handley Cross* the great sporting character Jorrocks, a Cockney grocer. Relations were forged on horseback which might otherwise never have taken place. Respect of spirit was mutual, and help in distress universal. In the quest for speed, in tandem with the rise in popularity of racing, fox-hunting soon succeeded hare-hunting with harriers: throughout all suitable country districts, mainly those without large acreages of arable crops and plough, packs of hounds proliferated.

By the 1870s the Billesdon country had lost many of its wooded patches and Mr Fernie spent much money and effort in making new coverts with gorse. His huntsman was a great exponent of the art and created Tamboro Hill in ten years: the covert, said never to draw blank, later became completely tree-covered from natural regeneration. *Nimrod's Hunting Tours* states:

'Independent of the pleasures arising from the Chase, I have always considered a covert's side, with hounds that are well attended, to be one of the most lively scenes in nature; and I have no hesitation in adding, that the best introduction for a young man of fortune and fashion of the present day is to be found at Billesdon Coplow or Cadby toll-bar.'

Some countryside became criss-crossed with the ditches of drainage works together with fences of small grazing holdings; the frequent obstacles giving rise to the name of 'pewey country' from their similarity to rows of church box pews. Nevertheless, once formed, the preservation of hedges, ditches and coverts became paramount in fox-hunting areas.

The rise in popularity of fox-hunting coincided almost exactly with the final wave of the enclosure movement at the end of the eighteenth and the early nineteenth centuries. But for enclosure by hedges and the obstacles that these produced, fox-hunting might never have become such a challenging and enduring sport. There are still many such hunting coverts spread across the Midland landscape which have led a dual life. While often recognised for their beauty, their historical and sporting associations have sometimes been forgotten. Without them the flat land would be even more barren.

The partridge – the bird that created shooting flying

The partridge also aided the development of the modern game gun more than any other bird. As agricultural England reached the middle of more than two hundred years of enclosure, the hedgerows of 'modern farming' abounded, providing even better habitat for partridges and, to a lesser extent, pheasants. The grey partridge (*Perdix perdix*) is native to Britain, and so was completely suited to our climate and island environment, at least until the last three or four decades. It thrives best on the lighter soils, on mixed or arable farms, where the fields are interspersed with hedgerows, copses and scrubland. Partridges were originally hunted for food, and taking them by netting and hawking were regularly practised until the game gun came into general use for shooting flying.

About 1705 Lord Townshend, the farming landowner of Raynham Hall, Norfolk, began experimenting with turnips as a sheep feed crop, inevitably earning the nick-name 'Turnip Townshend'. On the very poor light soils – to avoid a wasteful year of fallowing – he rotated turnips, corn, grasses and clover so that the turnip leys provided winter feed for sheep and cattle, thus returning more manure directly to the land for the following cereal crop. The historian Arthur Young (1741–1820) wrote of Townshend's land improvement:

Walking-up partridges in the enclosed farmlands with a variety of pointers. The picture shows the pattern of the corn, grass and turnip rotation. Dean Wolstenholme Snr.

Above: 'The Setting Dogg & Partridg's' – showing the action of primitive netting on the tamer partridges of those days. From *The Gentleman's Recreation. Right*: 'Common partridge, red-legged partridge and quail' from *British Birds* (1914). Archibald Thorburn.

'Thirty years ago it was an extensive heath, without tree or shrub, only a sheep walk to another farm. Such a number of carriages crossed it, that they would sometimes be a mile apart in pursuit of the best track. Now there is an excellent turnpike road, enclosed on each side with a good quick-set hedge, and the whole laid out in enclosures and cultivated on the Norfolk system in superior style. The whole is let at 15s. an acre, ten times the original.'

Partridges were to thrive in these new conditions and the growth in their numbers led to the increasing popularity of shooting, which by now was far ahead of hawking, as enclosure and cultivation divided up what had been a bare, often scrubby and inhospitable landscape. All the new crop rotations together with the draining and ploughing-up of downland, moor and heath benefited the wild partridge. When the corn was hand-scythed the tall stubbles were ideal, providing food and cover for the partridges. The same period also saw a reduction of the fox population due to the success and wide-spread following of 'modern fox-hunting' – some areas having to resort to importing animals.

Early shooting with muzzle-loading guns was assisted by the use of setters and pointers in walking-up fields of roots and high stubble. The dogs could wind and point the position of a covey of partridges, as if mesmerising them while they squatted immobile in cover. Our ancestors generally went out in pairs: when the game was located the guns would be cocked; one man would fire at the birds sitting while the other loosed off as soon as he saw the flash of the pan or heard the report. Such birds would just be flying, but shooting them was a difficult and sometimes dangerous feat with the long barrels, slow ignition, black powder and irregular pellets of early fowling guns. One can easily understand how the expression 'just a flash in the pan' came into use when guns failed to shoot after all the preliminaries of muzzle-loading.

Another early accessory occasionally used was the stuffed stalking horse or a jaded old farm horse, behind which the hunters hid until they got close enough to shoot the birds on the ground. Hardly sporting, sometimes frustrating, this was essentially fowling for the pot, using guns rather than the nets and springs of previous ages.

Many shooting pictures show sportsmen out with their muzzle-loading guns, more often than not with setting-dogs (setters) or pointers. These dogs, particularly the setters, had originally been trained to range out and indicate the position of coveys for netting. The dogs which were a mixture of spaniel and pointer would set the partridges, by lying still on the ground nearby to distract them while a long net was taken round in a circle until it was finally spread and put over the birds. Pointers were more generally favoured when walking-up shooting came into vogue.

After a long period of shooting at game birds sitting or perching, it became a challenge to shoot partridges on the wing as was the custom in France. This also meant picking a particular bird to shoot at, rather than 'browning' the denser part of a covey, which sometimes gave two birds with one shot. But two technical developments to guns and ammunition made towards the end of the eighteenth century enabled shooting flying to spread rapidly: the invention of the patent breech providing a faster and more powerful explosion, and the manufacture of regular sized and graded pellets made from lead dropped into water from a shot tower. Both developments produced better shot patterns and allowed barrels to be considerably shortened to around thirty-three inches and so more accurately bored, which made them less likely to explode. But it also gave a better balance to the gun and helped to prevent 'muzzle droop'. However thirty-nine inch barrels were often recommended for shooting in open farmlands after Michaelmas when shots were taken at greater distances. Late eighteenth century pictures of shooting scenes show the guns being held with the left hand incredibly far back. But this is quite understandable as gun barrels

Above left: Two gentlemen with their pointers partridge shooting away from the urban manufactories. James Barenger.

Above: Partridge shooting at harvest time – one would shoot at a sitting bird while the other shot flying. John Cordrey (*c*1770–1825).

Left: Mr T. Reed and Mr T. Squires shooting in a root field on Cudnam Hills, Kent. G. Reed, dated 1823.

were likely to burst and blow off parts of the shooter's hand when badly loaded.

By now the quick curving and swerving flight of the partridge was appreciated more by the stylists. No longer was it acceptable for gentlemen to shoot game birds sitting or to fire at random into the middle of a covey. By 1800 many sporting pictures portrayed the shorter guns, sometimes with double barrels side-by-side, two hammers and two triggers, but still muzzle-loaded with all the attendant problems. Many sportsmen such as Colonel Thornton still preferred several single-barrel guns with loaders. But both he and Colonel Peter Hawker maintained a large armoury of weapons in their gun rooms to suit different game.

The invention of Forsyth's percussion system in 1808 led to the use of a percussion cap which replaced the flintlock as a faster method of firing the powder charge; now misfires were cut to less than one per cent. Shortly after this the Eley patent shot load was introduced, in which the pellets

A covey of driven partridges passing over flooded marshland. J. C. Harrison.

were pre-packed into a paper-covered wire cage. Both these inventions made loading faster and easier. By 1826 when Joseph Manton – the most famous of early gunsmiths – retired, sportsmen believed that the muzzle-loading gun fired by a percussion cap and shooting a prepared cartridge-load of pellets was the ultimate in accurate weaponry.

In the latter half of the eighteenth century the best sporting guns were made in Europe, particularly in Milan, Paris and Madrid. In *The Gun and its Development* W. W. Greener states:

'The productions of Milan enjoyed the widest reputation; even in France a Milan piece was thought of as highly as in England. Pepys in his Diary (1667) mentions that French sporting guns had a vogue amongst English gentry, also that a London gunsmith Truelock possessed considerable reputation . . .'

The Napoleonic Wars afforded the English gunmakers an opportunity to regain the supremacy from their European competitors. Joseph Manton is best remembered among the makers of the early nineteenth century as a talented gunsmith and inventor of numerous improvements, and was to open the way to a golden period of English gunmaking.

The shot and powder loads were now being varied to suit the different circumstances encountered in shooting and this led to a great deal of experimentation by the gunsmiths and by sportsmen such as Colonel Peter Hawker, who was an active game shooter from 1812 to 1853. Although he was badly wounded in the Peninsular War in 1810 his diary shows that he stalked and shot every available type of game bird and wildfowl, designing his own equipment as he went along.

The plentiful coveys of partridges were increasingly shot for sport from the last quarter of the eighteenth century. They had become the main game

102

'That sudden Twist' – the challenge of driven partridges. J. C. Harrison.

birds of the countryside, and were protected by a closed season from January 31st to the end of August: licences for shooting or taking game were introduced in October 1784. Partridge shooting was growing popular as a field sport for both the rural and the fast-increasing rich urban middle class.

French partridges are introduced

It was inevitable with the busy traffic of gentry and noblemen between England and France over many years that the French or red-legged partridge (*Alectoris rufa*) would sooner or later be brought back to England by a keen sportsman. In 1673 several pairs of Frenchmen, as they came to be called, were introduced from Chambord to Windsor Great Park by Charles II, but within a few years they had perished. Almost a century later, in 1770, the Marquis of Hertford, whose family had been British Ambassadors in Paris, brought over both birds and eggs to his estate at Orford in Suffolk, and this stock survived. According to Daniel's *Rural Sports* 'many pairs of birds were introduced and many thousands of eggs which were hatched out under hens, and set at liberty at a proper age'. In due course other pairs were introduced on several estates in East Anglia: they flourished and gradually spread out to new areas in the eastern and southern parts of England. At first French partridges were unpopular with sportsmen, for when shot over pointers they would not obligingly freeze like our native breed until the dog flushed them, but crept forward stealthily and usually unseen. Later, when driven shooting took over, the redleg's value became more appreciated. But in flat country it was never quite the same challenging bird as the English grey partridge, and its habit of coming forward in twos and threes made it easier to shoot.

French partridge. Rodger McPhail.

The first agricultural depression after the end of the Napoleonic Wars lasted for some twenty years. Farm rents of low-producing and difficult arable soils in Essex, Cambridgeshire, Suffolk and parts of Norfolk were driven so low that shooting rentals in partridge country now provided higher returns for some farming landowners, still burdened by the earlier costs of clearing land for corn, and often more employment for local farming artisans in reshaping the belts and cover. Thus partridge shooting developed as a rural sport, attracting many people from the towns to the open countryside as they were made more mobile by the ever-increasing road and rail network.

Some prints show hunters shooting from horseback, with foot-servants in attendance for reloading; an anachronism somewhat similar to the procedure of hawking. But where the new modern farming was practised sportsmen soon dismounted to walk up with their dogs, the horses or ponies being retained to carry the bags of game. Partridge shooting soon became better organised in the open farmlands and as sporting guns improved, pointers, setters and spaniels were becoming better trained to their various tasks. Squires walked up their coveys with friends, loaders and dog-handlers. But other sportsmen, also, stood forward behind hedgerows, and thus the days of driven game started. It was soon developed by shooting men who were looking for ways of increasing the day's challenge with more difficult flying game, now crossing or approaching at speed and producing the more testing shots.

The concept of driving coveys over forward-standing guns was far-reaching and took many years to be fully understood. It needed a completely new approach and different skills. The muzzle-loading guns had to be loaded faster and more easily. Not for much longer could the use of two, or even four, loaders be tolerated – a practice necessitated by the laborious sequence of reloading. It was open to many mistakes and was extremely dangerous to both loader and shooter as a host of stories relate. The slow-burning black powder often led not only to loaders and guns setting their clothes on fire, or firing their ram-rods into the air, but also to volumes of smoke which obscured their view.

The driving of partridges was allegedly first tried about 1850 by Lord Huntingfield (1818–79) at Heveningham Hall in Suffolk. His keepers are said to have hurled potatoes over the high kitchen garden wall for his lordship's practice. Apparently he was a peppery old man in his later years and regularly went off to Monte Carlo for the pigeon-match shooting which was so popular with enthusiasts in the art of shooting flying. The new technique of driving was at first fiercely denounced by the old school, but steadily gained in popularity and by 1860 was all the rage. One of the earliest detailed bags of driven birds was made at Weston Colville near Newmarket between January 8th and 12th, 1860, when nine guns including General Hall and Lord Huntingfield – both crackshots – shot 1,077 brace. A main influence for the change was the introduction of the mechanical reaper which left the stubbles lower than the handscythe. This in turn made walking-up far less rewarding. By now the crop rotations were contrived to give better cover in both the breeding and the shooting seasons. Turnips and other root crops were grown for partridges, and later used as winter feed for sheep and cattle.

Hedges were allowed to grow taller so that sportsmen could stand back further from them. Evidence of this can still be seen around Newmarket, in many other parts of East Anglia and in the grain-growing lands of both Hampshire and Yorkshire, where long lines of wide conifer belts, mainly of scots pine, break up the flat countryside. These plantings, designed for pheasants as well as partridges, follow the hedge lines of earlier enclosures and divide what would have been a bare open landscape into more attractive and sheltered segments suited for game driving and shooting. While they are still a feature of the country, most have been neglected and have no bottom cover, so they are today relatively ineffective as game habitat – some have even become features in the urban spread.

The later developments to guns

At about this time the French gunmaker Casimir Lefaucheux had patented a sporting gun which 'broke in two' to give a drop-down system for breech-loading. It accepted an integral-cased cartridge containing its own ignition, charge and shot load. The single-barrelled gun was shown at the Great Exhibition in London's Hyde Park in 1851, and by the following year a London gunsmith, Joseph Lang, had brought onto the market a breech-loading gun. The seeds of breech-loading were well sown and the years of the muzzle-loader were now numbered, but early breech-loaders were often badly made and constructed with flimsy actions. Sportsmen in these early times still went out with both single and double-barrelled muzzle-loaders together with the new breech-loaders. By 1857 a few breech-loading hammer guns were being built in England or imported which shot the new composite, ready-primed pinfire cartridges and could be reloaded as fast as the cartridge could be inserted. By 1861 some further refinements of the game gun had been developed, incorporating a safer centre-fire cartridge with a hammer action gun: these were soon being made by most of the best Birmingham and London gunsmiths. This removed many of the objections of the earlier systems and brought guns to a new degree of safety, while greater accuracy was to be provided by carefully bored and better choked steel barrels. All the time improvements were being made to gun actions and a deluge of designs were patented. The particular period is confused by the variety and change constantly occurring to guns and cartridges, which is outside the scope of this book. In *The British Shotgun 1850–1870* I. M. Crudginton and D. J. Baker conclude that:

'. . . based on a study of such gunmakers' records as they have seen that, prior to the 1858 trial there were no more than a couple of hundred British-made breech-loading shotguns in the whole of the British Isles. But by the very early 1860s the total must have been several thousand. Among them was a pair of base fire Lancaster shotguns made for His Royal Highness the Prince Consort in November 1859.'

It was therefore not until the early 1860s that the art of driven shooting and the development of faster-shooting and safer guns really came together with the rearing of pheasants, and the care of woodlands. In the new Victorian scene of driven game, partridges were upstaged by the higher and faster pheasants for a period of fifty years. By the end of the century both had resumed positions of differing importance, while their virtues as game birds and table fare were debated whenever shooting men gathered together.

The pheasant – and driven shooting in the Victorian century

Before pheasant shooting came into vogue, they had been netted in various ways along with woodcock in the woods and copses, and in earlier times taken by the larger hawks when they strayed into open ground – but in most parts of the country they were fairly scarce. In fact this is illustrated by an extract from the Vernon papers covering Hanbury Hall, Shrawley estate, Worcester, where the combined bags for the 1754 and 1759 seasons

Woodcock shooting in thick undergrowth – not unduly attractive to gentlemen used to riding across the countryside (detail).

Two gentlemen shooting pheasants in a mixed wood with dense undergrowth. Dean Wolstenholme.

averaged 215 partridges, 83 woodcock, 122 snipe and 9 hares, but only 3 pheasants.

Thus it is not surprising to find that the only specific mention of pheasant shooting in *The Sportsman's Dictionary* of 1785 relates to the shooting of woodcock and pheasants, and the use of hardy spaniels to spring the game from thick cover in woodlands. From this it might be inferred that such shooting was a fairly toilsome pastime, not unduly attractive to gentlemen used to riding across the countryside. Probably if the undergrowth had not been thick and difficult to walk through at this time, the birds would have run forward for ever – giving little chance to shoot as they were walked-up.

But it was soon realised that the pheasant was a game bird which could show different sport in coverts, and at a later time of the year than provided by the partridge. The sophistication of Manton's muzzle-loaders

then later the breech-loader, was another key to this development of shooting flying; that of *driven* pheasants – now often reared – out of coverts.

The *Sporting Magazine* of 1805 throws interesting light on the art of shooting flying at that time showing these fines as displayed in a shooting lodge in Sussex:–

A sportsman shooting woodcock in a wooded river landscape. Abraham Cooper (1787–1868), dated 1859.

Woodcock. Rodger McPhail.

	£.	s.	d.
Shooting at a pheasant on the ground or in a tree	1.	1.	0.
Shooting at ditto at more than 40 yds. unless wounded		5.	0.
Killing a hen pheasant	1.	1.	0.
Shooting at a hen pheasant		10.	6.
Shooting two or more partridges at one shot		10.	6.
Shooting at partridges on the ground	1.	1.	0.
Shooting at partridges at more than 45 yds. unless wounded		5.	0.
Shooting a hare on her form		5.	0.

Woodcock had, in fact, been more plentiful than pheasants in most woodlands throughout the second half of the eighteenth century. In many areas

Ring-necked pheasant. Rodger McPhail.

A sportsman with his spaniel shooting in a wooded parkland very early in the season. G. Branscombe (c1785–1840).

they were often the main sport, together with ground game such as rabbits and hares. Woodcock – having different requirements – never attracted the same care of the woodlands as the pheasant. Nevertheless, the coppicing of many plantations which was widely practised in these times, improved the habitat for both species by breaking up the dense overhead canopy, providing skylights for the 'cock and letting in pools of sun for the pheasant. It also produced a variety of low regenerating vegetation and underwood. As regular records of shooting began to appear we have the modest totals of early bags of woodcock and pheasant – often in equal numbers.

In the agricultural depression after Waterloo, many areas with marginal soils became difficult to tenant. This resulted in them often being planted with mixed woodlands. These early nineteenth-century plantings, in parts of Buckinghamshire, Berkshire, Oxfordshire, North Hampshire and Sussex were later to provide additional coverts for pheasant shooting and some fox-hunting. Although the requirements are somewhat different they did produce a holding cover for foxes and also a lot of extra capacity in the form of coverts for pheasant shooting in Victorian times, as to some extent the pheasant had been driven to roost in the trees by the foxes, and had thus become more of a woodland bird. Those coverts that have been keepered and cared for by woodmen are still in good condition today.

Walking-up and driving pheasants

Modern pheasant shooting seems to have started in East Anglia. Lord Leicester, who had done so much to develop partridge shooting, soon appreciated the great possibilities of the pheasant as a bird of sport. From fairly early in the nineteenth century the famous coverts – like Scarborough Clump – in the park at Holkham, Norfolk – were shot on the regular plan which has been followed ever since. The principle of tapping the birds on into a woodland clump of holding cover, and then driving them back to the woods from which they had come, was one on which many good drives of pheasants in the country were later to be modelled.

The method of walking woodlands with a line of guns – as opposed to the driving of pheasants *out* of woods over the guns – was necessarily mixed with other techniques in the early days of pheasant shooting. There were estates then, as there are today, where the guns could walk through a deep wood – shooting while walking-up – so that the birds ran forward to the edge of the covert. When the last furlong was reached the guns would stand in a ride, whilst the beaters swung round and flushed the birds to them over the tops of the trees.

This approximate version of the modern system of driving seems to have started about 1829 on some shoots. Soon a small platoon of estate workers walked through the undergrowth towards the guns, who stood outside the woods to shoot birds which were flying higher and faster to other coverts.

Woodlands come in for much attention

Woodlands for pheasants were now laid out, planted and managed with a new vigour on most of the large estates. Covert shooting rekindled interest in woodlands which had died away as coal and the better transport services supplanted local timber for fuel, heating and firing the factories and mills. No expense was spared to improve old neglected woodlands by thinning or planting mixed trees and shrubs. No longer were they allowed to be draughty. New tree species were introduced and the outsides were often planted with attractive thick shrubs to keep out the winds. The art of designing flushing corners was developed, and plants like snowberry, now outdated, made their appearance for this purpose.

In parts of Britain, particularly in East Anglia, pheasants already thrived in the wild, but the other counties that provided good natural habitat were Southern Hampshire, Sussex, Hertfordshire, Shropshire, parts of Yorkshire, Derbyshire and some Scottish lowlands. A fashionable day's driven pheasant shooting now required a good weight of birds on the ground, and where this did not occur naturally estate owner, agent, forester and keeper worked together to improve the woodlands and the techniques for release after rearing.

The development of driven game shooting embraced many skills. All these were ready to be combined in the big shooting parties of the Victorian era, but two further elements were needed – mobility and patronage. The railways were to supply the first, and Royalty the second.

In the early 1860s the Prince of Wales bought Sandringham in Norfolk. It was to need many years and nearly £300,000 to transform it into a world-

110

famous shooting estate with the help of a neighbour, Lord Leicester of Holkham Hall. The Prince also built a railway station at nearby Wolferton, so that his guests and their paraphernalia could get up from London's Euston Station and back.

The railway companies responded by building more luxurious passenger coaches and the rail network expanded. House parties, so well described in J. G. Ruffer's *The Big Shots*, became the new social event of the period, and an invitation to three or four days' shooting on the country estates, the ultimate accolade. Immense fortunes were spent on the requirements of driven game – partridges, pheasants and later grouse. Royalty entertained and were entertained lavishly; the nobility and landowners followed suit.

As the Empire developed in the East, the opportunity arose to introduce different species of pheasants from Asia. Landowners vied with one another in importing both ornamental and sporting breeds from different parts of the world. Soon varieties such as Reeves, Golden, Silver and Lady Amhersts were to be seen flying over the guns – the owners always hoping they might have found a breed which was a better quarry, better eating and at the same time more beautiful than any shown by their neighbours!

A real proficiency in shooting was a passport to social success, providing almost continuous invitations to the famous shoots: Elvedon, Crichel, Hall Barn, West Dean, Euston, Six Mile Bottom, Great Witchingham and the rest. Now the day's bag assumed an unnatural importance, and for a time landowners competed with each other for numerical prestige. The guns, too, counted their birds with the accuracy of bank tellers, and there were occasionally hasty scenes of greed in staking claims to birds. As always, however, a new etiquette was soon established, effectively separating the gentlemen from the rest, and some delightful prose and loose verse was written to illustrate the nicer points of order. 'Better a bird spared than a bird shared' became the rule; and afterwards, when picking up game: 'Gentlemen, whilst upon the moors, don't say "that's mine – but here's yours".'

The Big Shots

As competitive owners vied for the honour of having the best shoots, both quality and quantity of birds grew more important, and this placed a premium on skill; the most accurate shots were regularly asked to join various parties. A number of people attempted to draw up a list of the twelve best shots in England during the last twenty-five years of the nineteenth century. Certainly most would include at the top Lord Ripon (the 2nd Marquis), Lord Walsingham, Sir Ralph Payne-Gallwey, Sir Harry Stonor, Lord Carnarvon, Maharajah Duleep Singh, the Prince George (later King George V), Lord Leicester (the 2nd Earl), Lord Ashburton and Mr R. H. Rimmington-Wilson.

Victorian ladies joined the scene, sometimes to shoot, but more often to accompany the party. With their recent return to the hunting field this recalled the customs of Elizabethan hawking several hundred years before. The shooting luncheon soon became a part of the day's sport comparable with the large food hampers that had always been taken to the races – unless a substantial meal was to be served in a lodge or marquee.

The new fashion for house-parties required the introduction of some extra variety, and often a three or four day programme would include an afternoon's duck shooting. Many estate streams and lakes were improved or created for this purpose – sometimes in a dry season an old reedy lake would instead produce a quite sensational pheasant drive.

One of the roles of the estate gamekeeper was the care, breeding and training of generations of the now naturalised shooting dogs: the pointers and setters used in walking-up to seek and point game for shooting flying, and the spaniels trained to flush or 'spring' game from the denser undergrowth in woods and marshes while being completely steady to fur. Neither had to give tongue, in contrast to the 'music' of hounds. As driven shooting spread, retrievers were needed for the separate task of recovering dead or wounded game, particularly from thick cover or water. But in 1814 Colonel

A shoot at Grimston Park, Yorkshire, 1868. The party is posed before lunch with a manservant opening champagne. The second from the right is Earl de Grey, the second Marquis of Ripon. Thomas Barker.

Peter Hawker, who lived on the Kennet at Longparish in Hampshire and also shot wildfowl on the tidal mudflats of the Solent, described the smaller variety of the Newfoundland as 'by far the best dog for every kind of shooting, is oftener black than any other colour and scarcely bigger than a pointer'. When the early Newfoundland dogs had been introduced there was some confusion as Colonel Hawker wrote: 'Every canine brute, that is nearly as big as a jackass and hairy as a bear, is denominated a fine Newfoundland dog.' From this it would appear that many varieties were being brought to England at an early date.

Throughout the nineteenth century men developed the St John's and Labrador breed of these animals, concentrating on this smaller of the two types with its soft mouth, good nose, ease of training and aptitude for finding game. Lord Malmesbury and Colonel Hawker arranged for many of the pure-bred dogs to be brought back to England in fishing and timber boats. Malmesbury, whose home Heron Court was near the port of Poole in Dorset, kept a shooting journal for forty seasons between 1798 and 1840. His bag including 10,744 partridges, 6,320 pheasants, 4,694 snipe and 1,080 woodcock. The import of Labradors continued until quarantine laws were introduced in 1895. Thereafter the breed became effectively established on English blood lines as the Labrador Retriever and by 1905 was the supreme dog for driven shooting.

A gentleman with his Newfoundland retriever on the outskirts of a large pheasant covert as the leaf turns. Thomas Bretland (1802–74), dated 1850.

The red grouse

The railways again played a part in opening up another sporting scene akin to pheasant and partridge shooting, as they enabled parties of guns to travel further afield to the moors of Yorkshire, the Border counties and Scotland to shoot grouse and blackgame. Previously, only where grouse were in reach of existing transport were they walked-up on their native moors. Colonel Thornton gives an early description in his *Tours* of 1784 in which he shot grouse, flew hawks and fished in Scotland for many weeks, living throughout in camp with his friends, servants and dogs.

Normally where the heather was old and dense grouse were difficult to find in quantity, but near the sites of small accidental fires or where sheep had grazed the heather in patches the birds were more numerous. In the 1840s a party of three or four guns, each with two or three dogs, might walk all day and return to their lodgings with six brace per gun.

It was learnt almost by chance that heather-burning could improve grouse stocks. The technique was tried out in about 1859 on the Duke of Portland's estate. Soon heather-burning on a rotation system was a routine part of moor-management, and with it came a more systematic attack on the grouse's natural enemies: particularly crows, wild cats, hill foxes and, unfortunately, some birds of prey. As early as 1858 a pamphlet was published by a Mr William Colquhoun, which quoted an observation by a Perthshire keeper four years earlier, who had noticed 'very small worms' in the intestines of grouse – obviously strongyles. The worms are referred to as 'strongles' and there is some muddled thinking about similar worms in the author's setter puppies, nevertheless it shows that in 1854 grouse disease

Purple heather. August in the West Riding of Yorkshire with a Labrador retrieving grouse.

114

The first grouse drive of the day with the beaters cresting the ridge. Rodger McPhail.

was being taken seriously. This information which was contained in Dr D. G. F. Macdonald's book *Grouse Disease*, published by W. H. Allen & Company in 1883 also discussed heather burning:

'One of the causes, then, of grouse disease is neglecting to sufficiently burn or mow extensive patches of the old rank heather in the best feeding-grounds, so as to ensure an adequate supply of tender heath-shoots for

Mr John Batsby and a friend with their pointers on the Yorkshire moors. The guns with no ramrod are probably early breech-loaders: together with the introduction of butts this would fix the date at about 1858–60. J. F. Herring Snr.

food, and cover for protection in winter and the breeding season. Old rank heather and decayed fibres lack the nutrition requisite for the healthy condition of the grouse, and are not duly assimilated in the system of the bird; disease of the liver results, of which they speedily die.'

Another extract contains advice that is relevant today.

'It is penny wise and pound foolish not to keep moors in as sound a state as possible . . . The principal means of effecting this is to judiciously drain the wet land and burn the old heather. Periodical heath-burning is absolutely essential to the well-being of grouse. Yet many gamekeepers are prejudiced against it. We are persuaded that the diminution of grouse by disease is in a great measure attributable to neglecting to burn the old heath. Grouse never hatch in long heather if they can avoid it, nor do they lie in it. Nests are rarely found in heather of more than a foot in length.'

Records show grouse 'driving' at Cannon Hall near Barnsley, Yorkshire, in 1805, but this was an isolated instance and was practised in a rough and ready way. Regular drives without butts were in vogue in Yorkshire by 1836, when three brace per gun per drive was a large bag. Lord Walsingham had adopted a modern system of driving to lines of butts on Blubberhouse in the 1860s, and on August 28th, 1872, shooting there alone with four guns (two breech and two muzzle-loaders) with two loaders he killed 421 brace.

As Scotland opened up for grouse shooting and wildfowling, many English sportsmen now had opportunities to stalk the herds of wild deer in the bare high grounds of the old forests. In the mountains they also discovered the wild ptarmigan (*Lagopus mutus*), a grouse-like bird which is pure white in winter: its plumage constantly changing through the year to become a mixture of grey and brown on its topsides in the summer months. As it lives in the rocks at around two thousand feet the ptarmigan is rarely seen and so enjoys a life of comparative peace from civilisation.

By the 1860s the grouse drives on the moors were adding an extra month or six weeks to the early part of the sporting calendar. This led into the partridge months on the farmlands after harvest, and then, as the leaf dropped, pheasant shooting would commence in the woodlands. The year naturally embraced other types of shooting such as inland duck. Coastal wildfowling was always a specialist pursuit, and, when punt guns were used, was generally more for the market place than for sport.

A red grouse covey scratching for food but alert. George Earle.

VI

Sporting Waters

Wildfowlers and the landscape

Wildfowling was originally practised – like all other forms of hunting – as a source of obtaining food. But in the earlier days of plenty the 'fowler was less concerned about conservation or habitat management than the hunter who shot mostly terrestrial game. Some hunters as long ago as Kublai Khan in the eleventh century had already realised that they obtained a richer game harvest if active steps were taken to apply simple husbandry methods to their quarry. In Cathay this had taken the form of planting millet and other grains in special food patches for the partridges and quail. Wildfowl and other migratory game did not come in for any special treatment.

  To be fair to the wildfowler in the early days – with his nets, decoys, snares and, as they developed, shoulder guns and punt guns – he was

Sportsmen duck shooting. Edward Duncan (1803–82).

simply harvesting a small proportion of a vast surplus. Conditions for waterfowl remained stable for somewhat longer than they did for birds trying to survive in the more rapidly changing landscape of ever more productive farming. Furthermore, game on the land was often more easy to concentrate and kill.

The first noteworthy species to disappear was the Great Bustard (*Otis tarda*), which last bred in England in about 1832, deprived of the undisturbed, open country of wild grasses or breckland by farm machinery and busy people. During the seventeenth century it was found in quite large numbers on the flat lands of Lincolnshire and Norfolk, but the almost prairie-like scenery which it loved and where it could see for miles in all directions, was gradually eroded by developments which brought farming and civilisation to these areas. The draining of the brecklands of Norfolk which subsequently made agriculture possible and the building of an elaborate system of ditches, dykes and inland waterways, together with the planting of trees to reduce the strength of the winds, broke up these areas sufficiently to upset the natural habitat of the bustard, which eventually became extinct. In Central Europe, where it still clings on today, silage cutting, spraying and the birdcage effect of electric power cables strung across its skies are inexorably reducing its numbers. In Spain quite high populations survive because some of the wilder regions remain unsuitable for agriculture. Change has not yet come.

In Great Britain, during the earlier periods of agricultural reclamation, when more land was being drained to be brought under the plough, it was only a domestic setback in terms of wildfowl. The vast areas of marshes, bogs and other wetlands that provided the breeding grounds for the hundreds of thousands of migratory 'fowl that visited our shores, were not yet affected on a scale that caused any noticeable decline.

The great bustard last bred in England in about 1832 – its habitat finally eroded by successive new farming developments. Print by Gould.

Commencement of a Cripple-Chase, after firing the 1st Shot into a Skein of Brent Geese & Tame Wild Geese

Wildfowling for Brent geese from punts at the mouth of the Lymington River, with the sand bar just covered by the tide. A composite by Col. Peter Hawker assisted by William Daniel R.A., c1820.

Now it is another story, but happily one in which international concern and co-operation are reasonably effective.

The hunter who shot wild fowl around the coasts had virtually no opportunity or incentive to improve the environment for his somewhat unpredictable and transient quarry. He could exercise restraint – but he could contribute very little else, for in most cases the land was not his to manipulate.

The inland duck shooter, on the other hand, having no special weather conditions, phases of the moon or tides to bring the 'fowl to him en route to feeding or resting areas, had to dam up streams, dig out flight ponds, flood meadows, plant up and otherwise improve bare-sided gravel pits – if he wanted to increase his bag of mallard, teal and snipe, or indeed in some places get any bag at all.

His creation of new waters – like the fisherman's – is modest compared to the special treatment of the landscape afforded by pheasant and partridge managers, but it is significant in quality. Even a pool half the size of a tennis court can become a haven for frogs, dragonflies, sticklebacks, newts, marsh and reedland birds, as well as rafts of starry white crowfoot flowers, yellow irises and other plants. In a very short space of time such places

The Wildfowler. Richard Ansdell.

Snipe shooting. A haven for marsh and water-loving birds, before the progress of farming and the management of rivers produced a tidier countryside. Samuel Howitt.

can become aquatic sanctuaries of great beauty, often providing breeding places for rare specimens of wildlife.

Flight pools have understandably been criticised because if they are overshot too many birds from a resident population can be killed. The responsible shooter will feed his ponds regularly to establish a flight, but he will only shoot them three or four times a season – resting them in between, but continuing the feeding. This provides a bonus for hundreds of 'fowl, particularly in hard weather, and in any circumstances helping the birds get through the winter in good condition for breeding. There are, of course, the greedy and the ignorant who do not show such consideration, but the weight of the bag consists mostly of our commonest species, the mallard, which at the moment shows no signs of decline. Another factor in their favour is that most flight ponds are dual-purpose: they also serve as breeding and overspill areas in the spring and early summer. On a national basis this vast network of man-made pools can only improve the habitat, also helping passing snipe and other waders.

This is not the place to discuss the management of such watery areas, except to say that a flight pond is very rarely successful if it is merely a

Geese at dawn on the Little Cathedral Marsh, Downpatrick. Peter Scott, 1935.

Clatworthy reservoir, Somerset. This beautiful, natural-looking lake has been made for Taunton's water supply and is a fisherman's paradise.

Larger expanses of water will sometimes be adopted by duck purely as resting areas, and even regular feeding with the most tempting barley will fail to get the birds to come in on an evening flight. It is best to fall in with the duck's wishes and maintain the water as a day resting place – making sure that it suffers the minimum of disturbance, and if necessary planting marginal cover and tree belts to ensure that it has as much shelter as possible. Sometimes an early morning flight will be taken: often the lake becomes a sanctuary. Sportsmen like to see the waterfowl on their property. neglected wet hole in the ground, left to become choked with 'bulrushes' (reedmace – *Typha latifolia*), Canadian pond weed (*Elodea canadensis*) and other such unwelcome colonisers. A pair of moorhens may be quite happy there, but for more interesting waterfowl a little care is needed. For instance, apart from considerations of food and cover, experienced sportsmen will never let ponds freeze over completely: in hard weather they will always ensure that duck and other birds have access to some open water.

The field consultants of The Game Conservancy are always saying that although wildfowl are usually put last on the list for any attention by the shooting farmer, they generally require it in the end. Initially an owner will ask for advice on the birds that will give him the quickest return.

Duck shooting. Print by Samuel Howitt.

These used to be partridges, but for some time now they have been pheasants: so the coverts and smaller woods are inspected and improved, new plantings made, game crops sited, birds reared and so on. Some increased sport can be guaranteed, and the capital value of the farm is increased. Two or three years later the grey partridges – always less predictable and slower to respond in these days of clean farming and seemingly a succession of cold, wet Junes – will be given some thought.

Lastly it is the turn of the ducks. A bulldozer or excavator is coming to the farm to undertake some other essential work and the owner wonders whether an old, disused pond can again be brought into use or an insignificant stream broadened out into a spacious pool. Thus some new waters are added to the property, new species start appearing in the game book and *Canard à l'orange* from the home farm makes its appearance at the table.

Sometimes pools are constructed primarily for utilitarian reasons: little reservoirs of water for fire-fighting being dug out in vulnerable plantations. They can usually be adapted and enriched to suit wildfowl without great difficulty, and the wood becomes a much more attractive place to visit. A new dimension has been added to the trees and diversified the once rather monotonous ecosystem.

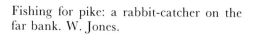
Fishing for pike: a rabbit-catcher on the far bank. W. Jones.

Anglers and their environment

The creative efforts of our anglers have made a much smaller impact on the pattern of the countryside in terms of mere acreage, but the new waters which they have contributed are aesthetically every bit as significant as the changes made by game shooters and foxhunters on farm and woodland. It is hard to know where this contribution began. The origins of freshwater fishing as a sport are not clearly documented, but the Rev. W. B. Daniel in *Rural Sports* (1802) claims that 'angling, or the taking of fish with a rod, hook and line, is said to have been practised 1498 years previous to the Christian Era'. Although he does not relate the source of this date. Fly fishing is certainly mentioned by the writer Aelian at the beginning of the third century A.D. when Roman soldiers are described catching trout on the river Astraeus in Macedonia. Local fishermen, having observed how the fish rose greedily to take a very small, wasp-coloured fly (*hippouros* or horsefly) when it touched the surface of the water, soon started to make up artificial flies.

'They wind crimson wool onto a hook' the author stated, 'then attach two wings (*ptera*) waxen in colour, which are taken from the neck feathers of a cock.

Using a six-foot rod (*kalamos*) and a line of the same length, they cast out their artificials, and the fish, attracted and maddened by their colour, rise freely, supposing from the pretty sight that a delicious mouthful awaits them. When they open their mouths, though, they become hooked and, caught, enjoy a bitter meal.'

Aelian described some of the materials they used for what he called 'hook fishing'. These included different coloured – presumably dyed – horsehairs, red and blue wool, and 'white, black and multi-coloured wings'.

This must surely be one of the earliest references to fly-fishing and fly-tying. Another Roman writer and poet described fishing on his farm in Spain and the thrill of 'playing a fish leaping on the end of your trembling line'.

Other Roman writers described rods of 6 to 8 feet coming from the reed-beds of Lower Egypt. Lines were mostly of twisted horsehair or flax, leaders of white horsehair, and hooks of iron or bronze, occasionally of bone. Some waters were reserved for private fishing and penalties for poaching were severe! We read of conservation practices just beginning. Perhaps there was also a slender link between fish farming and fishing for fun. Fishponds were known in India at the time of Buddha in around 500 B.C., and in Britain centuries afterwards the monasteries constructed stew-ponds and other artificial waters as fish-breeding and holding areas for fresh food. The eleventh-century records from the Abbey of Ely show that the Monks were liberally supplied with eels from such sources.

Earlier evidence from one or two Roman villas proves that stone-lined fishponds were dug out for their owners, just as they were in their home country where lampreys and tench were the commonest species kept. We know very little about this aspect of life in Roman Britain as fish bones are rarely found as well preserved as those of animals. However, in addition to sea fish, the remains of perch, eels and gudgeon have been identified from archaeological sites: some presumably from fishponds, others taken from local rivers and streams. We cannot pretend that these activities were connected with sport, but there would surely have been a day when an off-duty legionary or a Belgic slave surreptitiously baited a hook and pulled out a wriggling lamprey.

In Britain, Abbot Aelfric's *Colloquy*, compiled about the end of the tenth century as a textbook for his pupils, refers to 'throwing out my hook and my baskets' as well as the netting of fish in the river. The species listed in his catch included eels, pike, minnows, bull-heads, trout, lampreys and 'whatever else swim the river'.

In mediaeval and Elizabethan times almost every castle moat was used for the secondary purpose of breeding fish, partly for everyday eating, but more particularly as a source of food in times of siege. Similarly most manorial estates maintained ponds for food production. Carp was introduced in the fourteenth or fifteenth century – the first reference to it in the United Kingdom dates from 1496 – and was apparently enjoyed when doused with spicey sauces and tracklements. Fish was necessary as a religious observance on Fridays and fat carp were a source of considerable revenue. Pike were also farmed, and villagers were paid a farthing or two for a basket of frogs to feed them on. Some of the old fishponds are still in existence: now little more than historic relics, but attracting a few wildfowl as well as providing homes for fish. Their numbers are small, and their value today limited.

The progress of fish culture and angling meanders on through long-forgotten literature until the famous *Boke of St Albans* written by Juliana Barnes (*alias* Berners), allegedly Abbess of Sopwell Nunnery although proof is totally lacking. The book was produced in 1496, and whoever the writer was, he or she thoroughly understood angling as a sport. Much of the same information was set out in Leonard Mascalle's *A Book of Fishing with Hooke*

The common carp (*Cyprinus carpio*) and a moated scene where they were often kept in early times. The carp was introduced into England in the 14th or 15th century; the earliest reference to it dates from 1496.

Opposite
Top left: The stream is full of wild trout. Fishing the Wallop brook, a tributary of the Test, near the village of Nether Wallop. *Top right*: Fly fishing on the River Itchen near Alresford, Hampshire. One of the country's most famous chalk streams: managed and preserved with care and skill. *Above left*: Fishing the River Itchen for brown trout, near Winchester, Hampshire. *Above right*: Chub fishing: the Weir Pool at Throop on the Dorset Stour.

River landscape with anglers pike fishing. A. F. Rolfe, dated 1873.

& Line of 1590, which also showed that the skills of stocking and preservation had begun to be transferred from the stewponds to the rivers. .

The angler, of all different types of sportsmen, has perhaps shown the closest appreciation of his surroundings. Predictably we quote Izaak Walton, whose *The Compleat Angler* was published in 1635: 'I could sit quietly looking at the water, see some fishes disport themselves in silver streams, others leaping at flies in several shapes and colours. Looking at the hills, I could behold them, spotted with woods and groves; looking down on the meadows, I could see a boy gathering lilies and lady-smoks. . .'

Over three centuries later a feature writer in *The Sunday Times Magazine*'s article 'Down by the waterside' (July 1978) wrote: 'Water nourishes the landscape and our perception of it. Its many moods enhance and beautify, its many movements work unremittingly to shape and influence our scenery. Moreover, it captures our imagination and lends purpose to our leisure'.

Country sportsmen have always taken pleasure from such green and tranquil scenery as described in *The Compleat Angler* and have tried to preserve it. If it had not been for the interests of the so-called coarse fisherman many an insignificant little farm pond in a remote field corner would have been filled in. Flying down the whole length of England by helicopter on the Sunday after the Scottish Game Fair in 1978, we were surprised to see the number of quite small ponds – particularly in the North – often being fished by two or three people, sitting contentedly under their green umbrellas. Bulldozers would not have been welcome here.

The management of water changed through history, just as did land use, bringing benefits to some and problems to others. The development of water mills had an effect on the rivers and their levels, often creating deeper pools which helped the anglers. In time this interest in controlling the flow of water became related to the habitat demands of the fish and the sporting requirements of the fishermen. Naturally agreement between water board officials, mill managers, bankside farmers and anglers was not always reached. Just as with intensive agriculture and wildlife interests, there were two different extremes to consider; the water engineer's river – virtually a straight, easy to maintain canal rushing out to the sea – and a wandering stream of great beauty appreciated for its trout fishing, like the famous rivers Test and Itchen in Hampshire.

There can be no doubt that valuable salmon and trout fishing, in particular, has been and fortunately is still the reason for maintaining many of the river valleys in lowland Britain in a beautiful state. Slower moving rivers – like some of those in the eastern counties which are not very productive for game fish – have been straightened, deepened, and had the vegetation removed from their banks to lower the water table and improve the drainage for the surrounding farmland.

Today, with little or no need for the weirs and sluices which used to provide power for the mills and the mechanics for drowning watermeadows for an 'early bite' of grass, if it was not for game fishing interests, many more river bottoms would be dredged out and the water table lowered so that the rich land on either side could be cultivated more satisfactorily for arable crops.

In our Hampshire Avon valley one immediate effect of this would be the disappearance of the flock of whitefront geese from their wintering grounds at Somerley. And many other winter migrants – wigeon, teal, snipe, woodcock, would be greatly reduced in numbers.

Not only are so many sporting waters kept in an attractive state by the fishermen – and enjoyed by all who walk beside them – but they are also kept as pollution-free as possible. Clean water is of the greatest concern to the riparian owner. Early in the present century British anglers formed the Pure Rivers Society to try and influence legislation to deal with contamination problems. More recently, in 1948, it was another angler who

Lake fishing in Surrey.

formed the Angler's Co-operative Association whose main object was more or less the same – that of controlling water pollution.

As many more people go fishing than watch football matches, their interests are not without importance.

During the last twenty years the problems of dying fish in our polluted River Thames produced a dramatic story, as set out in Alwyne Wheeler's *Thames Trout and other Fishes* (Port of London Authority 1971). By 1957 the London Thames water had no fish living in the 40 mile urban stretch except eels, owing to insufficient and old-fashioned sewage treatment plants, as well as the enormous increase in synthetic detergents. It was too heavily polluted: the water black and anaerobic. However, in that year corrective measures were started, and biologists have been regularly monitoring the improvements ever since. (See K. E. Waite, Port of London Authority correspondence 1978). The anglers were not, of course, the only people who had been concerned. Now at least 96 species of fish have been recorded in the once lifeless water, and now duck and wading birds have also returned in force to our cleaner Thames.

The great River Rhine, by contrast, has probably become far too polluted ever to recover. It is a dead river, never again to give life to fish. There the man with the fishing rod was not powerful enough to argue with the interests of Industry.

In Britain we have also poisoned some of our smaller waters near industrial towns, but fortuitously by way of compensation the gravel industry has been creating new waters. These and other industrial holes in the ground have been adapted to provide fishing – both for trout and coarse fish.

On farmland, because of the increasing use of irrigation, water conservation has become necessary and special reservoirs have been constructed. Excessive water extraction during the summer levels would seriously affect the flow of rivers and streams, so it is logical to store water in the winter rather than let it escape wastefully to the sea.

Many of these irrigation reservoirs – fifteen to twenty acres in extent – are unfortunately still straight-edged and rectangular, with 2:1 graded banks kept bare of vegetation. We are always suggesting that farms should consider developing them as multi-purpose areas for both fishing and wildfowl, with the surrounding spoil banks landscaped and planted up as game remises and wildlife sanctuaries. The extra cost is negligible: the additional pleasure very great.

The huge water board reservoirs have been aware of the amenity side for a long time. Although these were on the whole constructed to provide water for a million or more utilitarian taps, the angler and the water authority have been quick to see that they can do business together. Stocked with fish, landscaped and skilfully managed, many of them are in time as beautiful as natural lakes. Except where necessary from an engineer's point of view we have seen the last of straight concrete edges. The earlier 'municipal bath' design is on the way out, or is at least well hidden. The more sensitive planners of today are happier to see bur-reed and purple loosestrife along the water's edge, and to hear the call of redshank and snipe.

VII
Designs for Game

The canvas upon which the hunter created his most lyrical effects of mixed woodlands and crop patterns that varied in size and texture was surely that of the English farm. Belts of trees and hedges further defined the mosaic appearance. It was, as we have said, largely the Victorians' interest in pheasants that first set the landowners to planting copse and covert. Earlier as Lord Townshend perfected his new system for the rotation of crops, the farms provided even more food and shelter for the partridges. The hedgerows that were planted as a result of the enclosures, and the changes in husbandry as the open field system was reduced – adding four and a half million acres to the land – further extended the better quality partridge habitat.

Shooting flying game from a steady cob: a method often enjoyed by elderly sportsmen not caring for too much walking-up. Thomas Musgrove Joy, *c*1850.

Towards the end of the eighteenth century the countryside was providing shooting that suited the comparatively primitive sporting weapons of the day. Wild partridges were almost there for the taking, thriving on the type of farming which provided insects, weeds and sheltering cover in plenty – without any special plantings. In 1797 the guns at Holkham Hall shot 3,800 partridges but only 396 pheasants.

In those days partridge conservation consisted mostly of preventing poaching and keeping down 'vermin'. Habitat improvement was virtually unnecessary. It was the pheasant that provided this extra impetus, inspiring sportsmen to design new coverts and adapt existing woodlands so that more and better birds could be shown.

The growth of pheasant husbandry has always been hard to trace as records differ radically from one estate to another. The accounts of Hatfield House mention the purchase in 1629 of 'hens to set on pheasants eggs' at one shilling each. We also know from a 1762 Act of Parliament that pheasants were habitually caught up and penned for breeding, and that by 1790 enough reared birds were being put to covert in certain areas to stimulate Henry James Pye to write his satyrical poem entitled *Amusement*, in which the gun 'covers the ensanguin'd field with home-bred game'!

Probably by 1800 a number of estates were rearing pheasants in quite a substantial way, and we learn from Scott, writing in 1820, that 'traders', i.e. the earliest game farmers, were supplying pheasant breeding stock. The game books of the period confirm that several estates were shooting a great weight of pheasants – all well documented in Hugh Gladstone's *Record Bags and Shooting Records* (1930). He records 1845 as being probably the first occasion when 1,000 pheasants were shot in a day by Lord Ashburton's shooting party of nine guns at Buckenham in Norfolk. It is, however, confusing to read that on some of the famous estates at much the same time, bags were still very modest. For example, on the Belvoir estate in December 1825 six guns shot only 22 pheasants and 2 woodcock. In the same wood ten years later, the guns, including the Dukes of Rutland and Wellington, killed 86 pheasants and other game totalling over 100 head. Still a relatively small bag.

We can only assume that rearing became fashionable at different periods in different parts of the country.

In 1837 Lawrence Rawstorne wrote his classic *Gamonia, or the Art of Preserving Game*, to which we have already referred. Pheasant rearing was discussed, but more importantly he wrote about planting coverts for game. His first chapter starts 'There has arisen of late years a great rage for planting, not only from that spirit of improvement which has displayed itself in adorning the mansions of the rich, but from the introduction of Battues, which require extensive preserves and numerous covers for the encouragement of game.'

Many of our ideas concerning venery – including Battues – came over from the Continent. In countries such as Bohemia enormous bags of mixed game were made as early as the 1750s. For example, Sir Ralph Payne-Gallwey, (Badminton Library, 1887) quoted a *chasse* lasting 20 days: 116,231 shots were fired by twenty-three hunters killing 47,950 head including deer, wild boar, foxes, a great many hares, partridges and pheasants – twice the number of the former – quails, larks and sundry other 'small

An attractive wild corner on a Surrey farm providing the cover and food essential for game, which soon vanishes when barbed wire takes over.

birds'. More than two head of game were killed for every five shots, so the shots themselves are not likely to have been very difficult ones, even allowing for the fact that some of the guests might have had six or more fowling pieces each, with the necessary loaders.

As far as one can understand the shoot was prepared – if that can be said to be the right word – many days in advance, when armies of men with dogs and nets drove vast tracts of countryside into a central wood or remise. The game – treading on each others toes, one imagines – was then prevented from escaping by high nets until the party was ready. As wild game was plentiful, it is probable that these huge bags were made without recourse to rearing.

Writers of the period tell us that as sporting guns became more efficient and accurate, such shooting went out of fashion. In 1888 Sir Ralph Payne-Gallwey himself describes two days sport of a different type in Bohemia, when 3,258 head of game was bagged by 11 guns. 'The birds were strong and wild and all shot on the wing. It is to be observed that none of the game was driven, nor any particular method taken to assemble it'.

A woodland shooting scene with the day's bag, after Stubbs. J. C. Ibbetson.

Planning for game: some aesthetic considerations

The importance of reared pheasants was two-fold. Firstly, it meant the sportsmen were able to enjoy good shooting in areas that were generally unsuitable for wild game production, because of a high rainfall, inimical farming and so on. Secondly, as the landowner had – in simple terms – to have somewhere to put the birds, thousands of beautiful coverts of mixed trees and shrubs were planted. The improved habitat for the reared birds also provided more cover for many other woodland species, and in some circumstances helped *wild* pheasants as well.

For a while the value of rearing was debased on both sides of the Channel – mainly during the Edwardian period – by so-called sportsmen striving for bigger bags than their neighbours. Today these unworthy *mores* have almost disappeared, except for a few insensitive, blinkered shooters who confuse quantity with quality. For the most part the glorious coverts and belts remain. The pheasant certainly made – and continues to make – a very important contribution to the beauty of the countryside.

In particular, shooting stimulates the planting of comparatively small areas, which would not be undertaken for purely commercial reasons. It also encourages the use of attractive hardwoods, in addition to – sometimes

Partridge shooting with a setter and a brace of pointers. In the distance are the pine belts that had become a feature of parts of the East Anglian landscape. Sam Alken.

135

instead of – the monotonous blanket of softwoods. Game requires a proportion of both – the pheasant formula for coverts of 'mixed species and mixed ages' creating most interesting effects. And with all the additional advantages of the well designed larger game covert, i.e. wide rides for maximum edge effect, and a grassy external ride to prevent the shading out of cereal crops – the habitat is further improved for a great many other wild creatures.

The advisory service of The Game Conservancy is continually helping owners to rehabilitate neglected woods, rather than clear-fell them: also to modify and beautify softwood plantations so that they will shelter pheasants and songbirds, instead of merely corvids and foxes. Current research is aimed at devising temporary herbage strips to replace hedgerows so that a block of open land may still conveniently and inexpensively provide some nesting cover and food for partridges and other birds.

The ways in which the landscape benefits from the attentions of the partridge shooter are to some extent more subtle than the changes effected by the pheasant manager. A ten acre wood sited above a steep valley is much easier to see and admire than the results of a farm manager's decision to curb the use of pesticides or his tolerance towards an overgrown marlpit.

The farm is, we know, the factory floor of the food-production industry and has to be efficiently managed. It must not, therefore, be over-run with perennial weeds and crop-destroying insects. Nevertheless, millions of acres of farmland which are shot over have been carefully planned, with partridges and other game considered as an integral part of the cropping programme. From a train window one can easily see the difference between the uncomprising 'food factories', and the game landscape – the one we prefer to live in, to ride over, to put on canvas.

Sir John Betjeman said recently: 'So many people think that beauty is tidiness, but Nature isn't tidy'. One has only to visit some of the collective farms of Central Europe or some of the cereal growing States in the U.S.A. to see what tidiness and straight lines do to the land.

The partridge shooter knows the value of a hedge – for cover and for driving – and is likely to consider carefully both sides of the argument before he orders in the bulldozers too hastily. A chalk pit in the centre of a field, filled with berried thorns, brambles, briars, willowherb, elders and wild grasses, makes the ideal sanctuary for a nesting bird. It is the cumulative effect of all these penny packets of cover that is so helpful to wildlife and makes our farms so attractive.

Even at the risk of a modern farmer thinking that we are living in the past we quote Gerard Manley Hopkins:

What would the world be, once bereft
Of wet and of wilderness? Let them be left,
O let them be left, wilderness and wet,
Long live the weeds and the wilderness yet.

The authors are not, in fact, living in the romantic days of carters in smocks and poppies in the corn. Our work takes us to farms all over Europe, to see how profitable farming can be integrated with good shooting. We have had many opportunities of seeing well run farms produce attractive sport, and

'Over the corner'. A covey of partridges – the game birds that did so much a few generations ago to preserve hedgerows and encourage the patchwork-quilt cropping of farms. Today, in many traditional partridge areas, they still help to check the rain of pesticides that destroy insect life – usually both the pest and the beneficial species! A partridge is still a useful barometer of the fate of many wildlife species. J. G. Harrison.

provide the kind of landscape that a Gainsborough would have enjoyed painting.

The winter months can be a hungry time for wild creatures on a modern farm, with stubbles burned and quickly ploughed in. In the partridge counties one will often see a careful disposition of the winter cereals: there will be some attempt to retain the varied chessboard pattern. Here and there mustard may be sown after the harvest. For the pheasants, three blocks of kale in different parts of the farm are more likely than one vast central block: patches of sunflowers, unharvested maize or canary grass will still be standing after Christmas and in this way one or two per cent of the land is allocated to the game enterprise.

Finally, there is the question of the rain of agro-chemicals that pours down on the crops to ward off bug or blight. In our opinion, much of it is unnecessary, ordered without sufficient thought – with only yield in mind rather than the net profit margin. Pest control is invariably undertaken

Poppies in a hedgebank – a rare sight today. Though it has often been said that 'a weed is only a wild flower in the wrong place', there is frequently no place in today's farm economy for little areas of untidiness so useful to wildlife. Effective game management, however, ensures that essential cover for nesting and other purposes is maintained across the landscape where it does not inconvenience the farmer to any great extent. And in these scattered sanctuaries we can enjoy our wild flowers and butterflies.

much more selectively by the farmer who likes to see the coveys whirring over his fields. The result is quite simply, not only more game, but also more butterflies and wild flowers. These are just the beginnings of a return to the palette of boyhood days, before England's fields were a uniform agricultural green.

New features in the landscape: gravel pits and reservoirs

Because of their sheer size the wet gravel pits and many of the newer reservoirs have made an immense contribution to the appearance of our countryside, as well as serving the interests of anglers mentioned in the previous chapter. Not so long ago 'gravel pit' was a dirty word, representing for a time dust, noise and streams of lorries. When the diggers departed a moribund or stagnant period followed and – often through no fault of the pit owner – many of the waste waters became a dumping ground for refuse and even old cars. In time Nature clothed the banks with plants and shrubs. Coot, moorhens, sometimes gulls, tufted and other duck would find sanctuary on the wet pits, and coarse fish begin to breed or be introduced by a local Angling Club. The resulting compromise would have been so much more productive and beautiful if the gravel authorities had planned from the very beginning with the co-operation of wildlife biologists.

Now we have a new generation of conservation experts, and fewer mistakes are perpetrated. As far as gravel pits and waterfowl are concerned great advances have been made.

One of the early pioneers in this field was the late Dr Jeffery Harrison, of the Wildfowlers Association, who was a distinguished amateur ornithologist. For many years he investigated the problems connected with this rather individual environment on a complex of wet gravel pits near Sevenoaks in Kent.

The Game Conservancy also mounted a major scientific effort, most generously financed by the Amey Roadstone Corporation, who built a specially equipped waterfowl laboratory beside a large study area at Great Linford in Buckinghamshire. Here there are both pits that have been worked out as well as ones where gravel is still being extracted.

We first became interested in wildfowl many years ago when one of the authors brought some reed nesting baskets back from Holland – a country that has managed wildfowl with considerable expertise for about four hundred years. The nesting baskets, originally used in commercial decoys, have more recently been adopted by duck shooters for increasing the numbers of breeding duck on inland lakes, and later in the season creating a lead-in for migrating duck. Mounted on stakes above the water, they provide protection from predators and give some shelter in extremes of weather.

Garganey dropping into a sheltered pool in May. Hugh Monahan, dated 1952.

An experimental gravel pit near Fordingbridge, Hampshire, used by The Game Conservancy for wildfowl studies. The banks have been gently shelved and are planted up with willows, alders, reeds and other quick-growing plants. 1966.

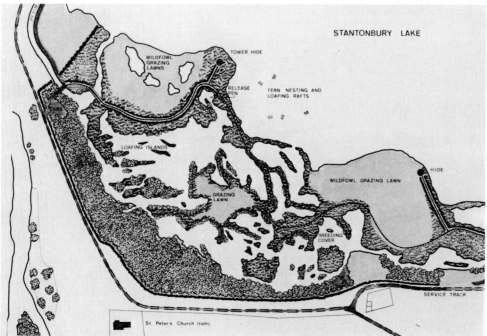

STANTONBURY LAKE

WILDFOWL GRAZING LAWNS

TOWER HIDE

RELEASE PEN

TERN NESTING AND LOAFING RAFTS

CARS

LOAFING ISLANDS

HIDE

WILDFOWL GRAZING LAWN

GRAZING LAWN

BREEDING COVER

SERVICE TRACK

St. Peters Church (ruin)

Stantonbury Lake, Great Linford, Buckinghamshire. The layout of the Amey Roadstone/Game Conservancy waterfowl reserve and study area. Many new features have been incorporated to improve breeding habitat. This makes an interesting comparison with the deer parks planted at the end of the 17th century (See page 12).

Four years later the cover was playing a vital part in providing some of the conditions needed for wildfowl and other wildlife species on what was once a bleak and inhospitable gravel pit.

On a disused 16 acre pit in Hampshire, which normally carried about five or six pairs of mallard, we found that with the aid of nesting baskets we could quickly increase the breeding density to over 30 pairs. By manipulating the timing of the hatching so that the weather would be more inclined to favour the baby ducklings, we succeeded in putting a great many extra broods on to the water. But most of them failed to survive owing to the lack of insect food. A gravel pit environment can be a hungry one. The waters tend to be rather deep and dark; sometimes the temperature can be on the cold side. After the gravel has been removed from an alluvial deposit the bottom of the pit is usually clay which is completely sterile of insect life and vegetation. Nature takes many years of successive plant and animal life cycles to enrich the base silt. Our research is aimed at accelerating this process.

The challenge we face is to try and plan the gravel digging operations so that the final water area will be productive – perhaps with a few islands for nesting accommodation, duck loafing sites and sanctuaries. Ducks need more than a sheet of water – however perfectly suited to their needs: the surroundings along the banks and beyond are equally important.

Of course, the hunter and the wildlife biologist cannot have it all their own way – gravel must come first. But modern gravel companies, unlike

Left: Nutscale Reservoir, Exmoor: the water supply for Minehead. It holds a good stock of brown moorland trout and some rainbows.

Right: Partners in a country sport.

Below: A farm near the North Downs at Bletchingley, Surrey. Modern agriculture utilises large machines which in turn require large hedgeless fields – of little use to game birds. Compromise is usually possible, though less easy after the hedges have been destroyed.

their predecessors, have a public conscience and are prepared to adapt their operations when necessary to suit the requirements of the waterfowl. Banks are gently graded, rather than left as steep cliffs inaccessible to baby ducklings, shallow 'wet shelves' are constructed close to the shoreline so that suitable aquatic plants will colonize and produce their share of insect food for the growing young. Here the temperature will be warmer and other bottom-living insects and crustacea will develop. Sheltered brood bays – providing privacy and calmer waters – can also be dug out speedily and at little cost while the heavy machinery is on the spot. Later it becomes too expensive. Back from the water's edge there must be suitable nesting cover, and beyond that perhaps some sheltering shrubs or tree belts, depending on how exposed the new lake will be.

We have achieved a great deal already, but there is still a long way to go. In time we hope to have a near-perfect blueprint for gravel companies who may wish to leave behind them an attractive wetland area with the right conditions for both wildfowl and anglers. Other landscaping skills provide what is needed for dinghy sailors.

At the present time some 2,000 acres of new waters are left after mineral extraction every year – a wonderful addition to our countryside amenities if skilfully managed.

Managing wildlife and game

The creation and maintenance of wildlife habitat is one of the first rules of conservation, but having established the necessary 'breeding areas' we must protect and manage them.

Most wild animal populations need this skilled management. If deer, for example, were not selectively culled according to age groups and other considerations, in areas favourable to them they would increase until they outstripped their food supply – at this stage damaging timber and farm crops to an unacceptable degree. In due course their population would crash due to starvation or disease. At one time natural predators such as wolves would have regulated their numbers. But now man has to fulfil this role in Britain. As an American wildlife writer, Fred P. Evenden of The Wildlife Society, explained recently: 'Most non-endangered wildlife species are somewhat like an apple tree. *You do not ruin the tree by picking its fruit, nor do you help it by allowing the apples to fall to the ground and rot*'.

National Game Park reserves in many countries depend greatly on their game wardens whose role is very similar to that of their British counterparts. A National Park without a managed wildlife regime soon becomes a playground for predators, and the variety of wildlife usually deteriorates. When this happens the whole area rapidly falls into a decline exemplified by the preponderance of a relatively small number of species.

The role of man as a 'hunter conservationist' is perhaps demonstrated in one of the wildest species of game birds, our red grouse (*Lagopus scoticus*). These birds live and increase freely on the heather moors so long as their habitat is properly managed.

The natural habitat of grouse is heather; its diet mainly heather shoots, with some grain, berries and insects. Left entirely alone – unburned and undrained – the age structure of this vegetation would get out of balance

The Earl of Sefton and party returning from grouse shooting above Meggernie near Tomintoul, Perthshire. When this picture was painted in 1841 the rail link-up from the South had not taken place: this happened in about 1847. The newly-invented breech-loading gun was not publicly exhibited until 1851. It was these two events that later on brought southern sportsmen to the Scottish moors in fair numbers. Richard Ansdell.

and the quality would decline quite rapidly, and so would the grouse. If it were not for the grouse about 10 million acres of the highlands of Scotland and the North of England would be unkeepered and virtually valueless, unless we completely changed the type of land use, and where possible, covered the ground with more softwood forests, and a different type of grazing for sheep.

There is little doubt that the traditional management of the moors for grouse shooting, maintains a most attractive environment, with a patch-work of variously-aged heather, plenty of purple bloom and – except where seriously over-grazed by stock – few tracts of dull, poor quality grasses.

If shooting were to be abandoned and the grouse and the heather left to their own devices, scrubby woodland would take over at the lower altitudes. This would probably consist of a mixture of conifers, silver birch, gorse, bracken and grass. Not a wholly unattractive landscape, but straggly, more shut in – like a thousand other areas of semi-waste land on the edge of golf courses, though wilder and more undulating. Something glorious – using the word intentionally – would have gone; the spaciousness, the wide horizons, most of all the unique seas of brilliant heather.

If sheep production was stepped up to more intensive levels, the heather would gradually disappear and we should be left with large areas of monotonous grey ground.

In a recent lecture, Dr Adam Watson of the Institute of Terrestrial Ecology, Banchory, referred to what might happen if grouse shooting was discontinued: 'The effect', he said, 'would result in a serious degradation of the scenery'.

Speaking of America's great game bird, the ruffed grouse, Professor Aldo Leopold once said: 'Everybody knows that the autumn landscape in the north woods is the land, plus a red maple, plus a ruffed grouse. In terms of conventional physics, the grouse represent only a millionth of either the mass or the energy of an acre. Yet subtract the grouse and the whole thing is dead'.

The relationship of the red grouse to our own northern moors is no different. It is not often realised that the greater part of a red grouse brood will fail to survive till the following season, whether they are shot or left alone. If not shot, two-thirds of the birds would simply be killed off by hunger, disease, stress or predation. It is because grouse are shot, that the moors are keepered and the heather carefully burned at appropriate intervals to provide the maximum number of breeding territories, cover for nesting, food and shelter, which ensure that the maximum number of birds are raised. Shooting harvests the surplus provided by careful management.

Throughout the world generally, wildlife species that are not classed as game and have not attracted the conservation skills of the hunter, have fared worse than those which are shot. The list of birds which have been hunted without becoming extinct is far shorter than the tally of those that have been exploited to extinction in one way or another or have died because of the changes to their habitat. 'Wildlife's great problem today', wrote American Ed Kozicky, 'is not controlled hunting but uncontrolled use of environment'.

We have always maintained that if the humble corncrake had flown like a partridge and tasted like a woodcock, there would be a few more of them about today.

The Capercaillie (*Tetrao urogallus*), a large turkey-like grouse, did become extinct in Scotland by 1771. It had originally been found in parts of England, Wales and Ireland, but by around 1670 it had become extinct in England. The main causes seem to have been the great diminution of its natural habitat by the slow destruction of the ancient pine forests, though climatic factors and disease may have assisted the reduction of numbers.

However, in 1837, the year Victoria came to the throne, the Capercaillie was reintroduced from Sweden to an estate on the Tayside. Within twenty five years there were at least one and a half thousand birds on this estate alone, and it has now been satisfactorily re-established and maintained throughout the mature pine forests of East Scotland for over a hundred years. During much of this time it has been culled by shooting to prevent local over-population and excessive damage to young conifers.

These examples show how man has to keep the animals and their habitat in balance with the pressures of so-called civilisation. The hunter plays a major part in maintaining this equilibrium, and in assisting wild quarry species in their struggle for survival against neglected woodlands, prairie farming, concrete coverts and toxic chemicals.

Though it may seen paradoxical to some, the shooting man makes a substantial contribution to the shapes, colours and textures of the landscape. Without his interest the countryside would much more rapidly become a regimented production area – devoid of hedgerow and spinney – strung about with barbed wire where stock was kept: an Orwellian concept already a reality in some countries.

Cock capercaillie – a bird that became extinct in Scotland by 1771, but was successfully re-established by sportsmen from an 1837 introduction of Swedish birds. Douglas Anderson, 1978 (detail).

VIII
Pressures
on the Countryside

The widespread reshaping of the countryside during the Georgian reigns and the masterpieces of scenic beauty which were the outcome soon became looked upon as the natural landscape. It was fortunate that this era coincided with the development of field sports and several golden periods of farming of the nineteenth century. Trees and hedgerows were planted in a manner best suited to the use of the land and in the long term the best interests of agriculture, forestry, field sports and communications.

But this warm, attractive countryside, with its patchwork quilt of textures and colours, is changing fast. And these changes are still being effected by people.

It seems pointless to repeat the well worn statistics of our vanishing green acres: the thousands of miles of hedgerow that have been bulldozed away, the vast areas of fields submerged under new buildings and motorways, the skylines that have taken on the shapes of rigid lines where once there were soft curves. People are bored with such facts, though they are not yet shocked by them. Perhaps this is because – compared to some of the more densely populated regions across the Channel – we are still fortunate to be able to shoot, fish and hunt in relatively wild and unspoiled surroundings.

But changes can be insidious and often come about almost unnoticed.

We were recently shooting in the Low Countries on an area of neat, intensively managed farmland. Almost wherever we looked container trucks were travelling across the horizon. Snipe and reared pheasants – for how could there be wild ones? – were silhouetted against factory chimneys; mallard circled in an industrial sky, shared with the vapour trails of Boeings. But our charming hosts seemed hardly to notice. Their planners and politicians had slowly but effectively strangled most of the traditional country sports: partly perhaps through misconceptions, partly because they had never taken the trouble to define and appreciate the hunter's concern for his countryside, going back over a thousand years.

The English landscape now faces the biggest changes since the enclosures began nearly 300 years ago. We have no wish – and it would be unrealistic – to try and arrest the future developments of our countryside in a state of glacial preservation. We must grow food and build houses. But in designing the landscape of the future, we should remember the Royal Society for the Protection of Birds' maxim 'Save a place for the birds', as well as that other injunction 'Plant a tree for posterity'.

To combine these two ideas we should also try to promote 'Save a place for the hunter', which would at the same time ensure a place for the painter of wildlife and landscape.

The countryside of the future was well considered by Nan Fairbrother in her book *New Lives, New Landscapes* published in 1970.

'The old countryside pattern will not disappear all at once. Some in fact is permanently inbuilt like the network of lanes, and the old villages with their magical old names; and even the vanishing field-pattern is a gradual dissolution which we gradually accept. There is a huge inertia in the countryside which delays all change needing positive action, and the old land-structure of small farms is still strongly entrenched. Also large areas of the countryside, especially in the most attractive places, still belong to the traditional large landowners who have always been concerned with amenity, and this continues to be an important factor in preserving the traditional beauty of our rural landscape.

Some woods too are likely to survive for generations still, and some hedges as boundaries and as barriers along roads (where human animals' will still be loose in the landscape and still need containing). Here we might retain or even replant the old flowery walls of hawthorn with all their hedge-bottom life.

The difference therefore between good and poor land which in the past was a gradation of merit is now becoming a difference of kind; and unless

'What comes through clearly is the vital part played by trees and hedges as the vertical green factor in our landscape. Trees help to blend groups of buildings into the countryside rather than merely hiding them.' Nan Fairbrother, c1970.

land can be improved to support mechanisation it is likely to be of little value for farming. Already in the uplands much poor land is abandoned, and the neglect is now swiftly and widely spreading to marginal land in the lowlands.

Whereas therefore the old landscape was a variation of farming intensities from rough grazing to arable, the future countryside is likely to consist of two distinct elements – open land intensively worked, and little-used areas eventually returning to woodland. It is an incipient new pattern already developing over hundreds of thousands of acres.'

Two distinct elements are predicted. If these two-land use types are extensive and sharply bounded, we shall certainly not enjoy travelling through the miles of open grassland, the barley factories and dark spruce forests, to get to our allocated playground areas of unproductive land, where we can presumably go rambling or picnic.

A proper consideration of land use requirements, including country sports, will avoid such polarisation.

The new landscapes must understandably relate to more industrialised or intensive farming and their texture will change over the years just like that of a garden. It cannot look the same as it did a hundred years ago; yet with understanding a transformation can be accomplished which need not be too drastic and which can preserve many of the old values. The new pieces of land patchwork will be of different shapes and sizes from those arranged by the earlier Enclosure. Already many landowners who have ripped out hedgerows – and even some of the institution farmers who do not live on their properties – are being persuaded to put back wildlife and amenity cover, perhaps in more convenient places to suit the new forms of cultivations.

Pressures on the countryside are increasing. The year 2000 may see a return to the position around A.D. 1650 – the period before the general enclosure by hedges, which also marked the nadir of the destruction of our forests and woodlands of which John Evelyn, the diarist, complained.

What comes through clearly is the vital part played by trees and hedges as the vertical green factor in our landscape. Trees help to blend groups of buildings into the countryside rather than merely hiding them; they join pieces of countryside together, and break up the skyline and the hard edges of farmland. Trees produce different colours, textures, silhouettes and shadows, which change throughout the seasons. A few acres of mixed trees and shrubs – not geometrically contrived – can make a scenic impact far greater than that of fifty acres of arable crop.

The English countryman has always cared about his surroundings – particularly our often oppressed landowners, so many of whom own quite small holdings and no longer vast estates. According to the Country Landowners Association the great majority of their members are owner occupiers of less than 300 acres each; half of them own less than 100 acres.

If the call of the partridge or the crowing of a pheasant, could be heard a little more clearly and a little more frequently in the fields of Westminster, our countryside might still be worthy of a Constable in a hundred years time.

150

The Cornfield. The lane leading from East Bergholt to Dedham across the meadows. Wrote Henry Phillips, a botanist friend of Constable, to the painter about this picture: 'I think it is July in your green lane. At this season all the tall grasses are in flower, bogrush, bulrush, teasel. The white bindweed now hangs its flowers over the branches of the hedge; the wild carrot and hemlock flower in banks of hedges, cow parsley, water plantain &c: the heath hills are purple at this season. . . .' John Constable, dated 1832.

Almost a Constable scene of the 1980s – albeit in Gloucestershire – depicting the warm cosy landscape that shelters wild game.

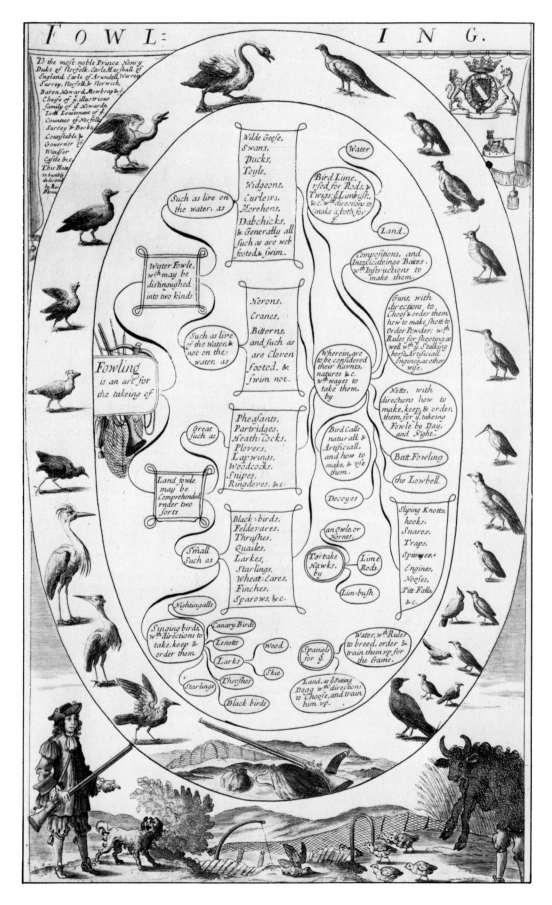

Fowling. From *The Gentleman's Recreation.*

Bibliography

After some consideration the authors have decided to include a short Bibliography – a full list could be endless, but these are some of the works we have consulted.

Nicholas Cox: *The Gentleman's Recreation* (1674) – 'Hunting'. Reprinted by the Cresset Press, 1928.

Rev. W. B. Daniels: *Rural Sports*; Longman, Hurst, Rees & Orme, London, 1802 and 1812.

The Sportsman's Dictionary; or the Gentleman's Companion for Town and Country; G. G. J. and J. Robinson, London, 1735, third edition 1785.

Delabere P. Blaine: *An Encyclopaedia of Rural Sports*; Longman, Green, Reader & Dyer, editions of 1858 and 1880.

Lawrence Rawstorne: *Gamonia or The Art of Preserving Game*; privately printed by Rudolph Ackermann, 1837. Republished by Herbert Jenkins, 1929.

E. D. Cuming: *British Sport – Past and Present*; Hodder & Stoughton, 1909.

E. Pollard, M. D. Hooper and N. W. Moore: *Hedges*; Collins, 1974.

George Mingay: *Rural Life in Victorian England*; Heinemann, 1977.

E. W. Bovill: *English Country Life, 1780–1830*; Oxford University Press, 1962.

J. H. Bettey: *Rural Life in Wessex 1500–1900*; Moonraker Press, 1977.

W. G. Hoskins: *The Making of the English Landscape*; Hodder & Stoughton, 1955; second impression, 1977.

W. G. Hoskins: *One Man's England*; BBC, 1977.

Book of the British Countryside; Readers Digest, 1973.

G. W. Turner, *Memoirs of a Gamekeeper*; Geoffrey Bles, 1954.

Charles Coles: *The Complete Book of Game Conservation*; Barrie & Jenkins, 1971 and 1975.

G. E. Freeman and F. H. Salvin: *Falconry – its claims, history and practice*; Longman, Green, Longman & Roberts, 1859.

Raymond Carr: *English Fox Hunting – a History*; Weidenfeld and Nicolson, 1976.

Roger Longrigg: *The English Squire and his Sport*; Michael Joseph, 1977.

Wilson Stevens: *The Guinness Guide to Field Sport*, 1979.

J. G. Ruffer, *The Big Shots – Edwardian Shooting Parties*; Debrett, 1977

Stella Walker: *Sporting Art – England 1700–1900;* Studio Vista, 1972.

British Sporting Paintings 1650–1850; Arts Council, 1974.

Walter Shaw Sparrow: *British Sporting Artists*; John Lane, The Bodley Head, 1929, republished 1965.

Col. H. H. Grant: *The Old English Landscape Painters*; F. Lewis, 1926; republished 1959–61.

David Coombs: *Sport and the Countryside*; Phaidon Press, 1978.

Col. P. Hawker: *Instructions to Young Sportsmen in all that relates to Shooting*; Longman, Rees, Orme, Brown, Green and Longman, 1814; seventh edition 1833.

H. G. Folkhard: *The Wild-Fowler*; Longmans, Green & Co., 1859.

The Badminton Library of Sports and Pastimes (edited by the Duke of Beaufort); Longmans, Green & Co., 1887.

Hugh S. Gladstone: *Record Bags and Shooting Records*; H. & S. Witherby, 1930.

W. W. Greener: *The Gun and Its Development*; Cassell & Co., eighth edition 1907.

I. M. Crudgington and D. J. Baker: *The British Shot Gun*; Barrie & Jenkins, 1979.

Countess Howe and Geoffrey Waring: *The Labrador Retriever*; Popular Dogs, 1957; republished 1975.

Charles Dixon with illustrations by Charles Whymper: *The Game Birds and Wild Fowl of the British Isles*; Pawson & Brailsford, 1893.

John C. Millais: *Game Birds and Shooting Sketches*; Henry Sotheran, 1892.

A. Thorburn: British Birds; Longmans, Green & Co., 1914.

John Marchington: *A Portrait of Shooting*; Anthony Atha Ltd. and The Game Conservancy, 1979.

G. M. Trevelyan: *English Social History*; Longmans, Green & Co., 1926.

Arthur Bryant: *English Saga 1840–1940*; Collins, 1940.

Nan Fairbrother: *New Lives, New Landscapes*; The Architectural Press. 1970.

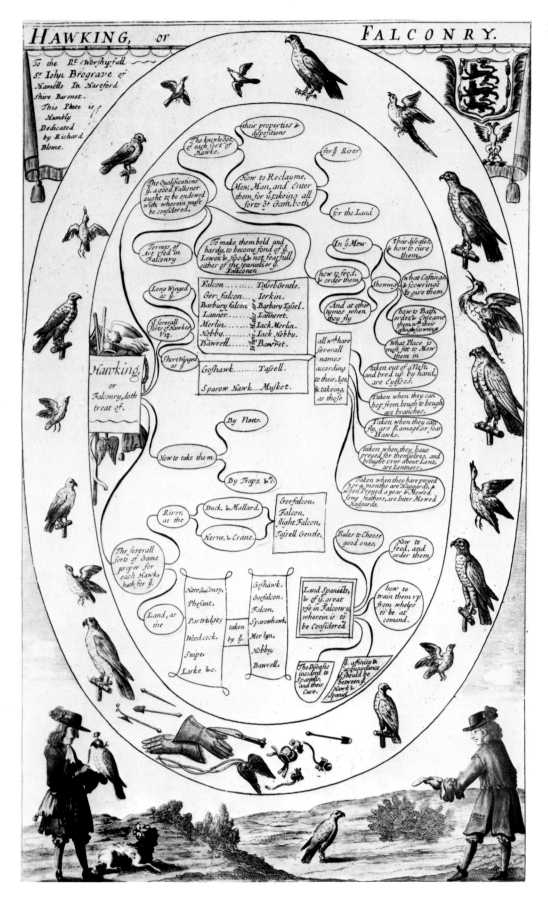

Hawking. From *The Gentleman's Recreation.*

Acknowledgements

It has not been easy to marshal together all the various forms of assistance that we have received over the three years that it has taken to compile this book, but we hope that no contributor has been overlooked.

The Council and Staff of The Game Conservancy, together with our President, The Duke of Wellington, have been a source of inspiration and a pool of information for a variety of topics concerned with the text. Regarding the selection of the pictures we have also received most helpful advice and assistance. Our thanks must go to Messrs Alfred Gates and George Welham of Ackermanns, and Peter Johnson of Oscar & Peter Johnson, who put at our disposal records of the many pictures which have passed through their galleries over decades. Equally, Sir Oliver Millar, the Curator of Her Majesty the Queen's collection, and Malcolm Cormack, the Curator of the Yale Center for British Art, opened their photographic treasure chests to aid the selection of the paintings we required. Our visit to Newhaven, direct from Concorde, coincided with a public holiday when the library was closed, but thanks to Malcolm Cormack and Joyce Guiliani we were given the free run of galleries for several hours, and a great deal of help. Stella A. Walker, whose book *Sporting Art – England 1700–1900* is now out of print, kindly read our draft chapter on this subject and made many suggestions which were gratefully appreciated. Messrs Spink & Sons Ltd., Malcolm Innes and Partners Ltd., Baynton Williams Ltd., David Messum Ltd., The British Sporting Art Trust and The Tryon Gallery Ltd. also co-operated willingly in providing prints and paintings. Rodger McPhail, complying with a last-minute request, generously made some scraper-board sketches for the decoration of a number of pages.

Michael Clayton, editor of *Horse & Hound*, and Peter Johnson, past Chairman of The British Sporting Art Trust, were more than helpful in suggesting sources of information and in reading early drafts of both the hunting and sporting art chapters. Our thanks must also be recorded for the criticism and advice given by Mrs Frances Roos and Mrs Jane Burditt – both from New York – who independently read some of the earlier historical material – giving us the benefit of their experience in editorial matters. We should also like to thank our secretaries Betty Saunders and Wendy Smith who typed and photo-copied the early manuscripts so many times that they now need new typewriters and reconditioned copiers.

We feel that the photographs also provide a necessary complement to the pictures and prints. Kenneth Scowen and John Tarlton obligingly sorted through thousands of prints to find those that fitted our requirements.

Due recognition must also be given to the many earlier authors who painstakingly researched subjects as diverse as social and agrarian history, the development of country estates, sporting art, game management, field sports and many other rural pursuits. They were an essential part of our jigsaw puzzle.

C. A. V. and C. L. C.

Illustration Sources

Where there is more than one illustration on a page, each is here distinguished by letters 'a' to 'd' in sequence from left to right and top to bottom.

Her Majesty the Queen: 16b, 25, 60a, 60b

Arthur Ackermann & Son Ltd.: 18, 27b, 27c, 30, 35, 40, 41, 56a, 56b, 58a, 59, 65, 66b, 67b, 69, 70, 71, 76a, 80, 81, 83, 84, 86a, 86c, 91, 92b, 93, 94, 95a, 95b, 96, 100a, 101, 107, 108, 114a, 115b, 117, 120b, 121, 126b, 134

Aerofilms Ltd.: 16a, 51

Amey Roadstone Corporation: 140b

Baynton Williams Ltd.: 12, 13, 14

The British Museum Library: 22b, 29, 33, 43, 77, 99a, 118, 152, 154

The British Sporting Art Trust: 8, 106

Nan Fairbrother: 148

Frost & Reed Ltd.: 75a

The Game Conservancy: 44, 140a, 141

The Trustees of the Grosvenor Estate: 62b

Malcolm Innes and Partners Ltd.: 39c, 73

Oscar and Peter Johnson Ltd.: 6b, 6c, 20a, 20b, 26, 27a, 36, 39a, 52, 55, 62a, 66a, 67a, 90a, 92a, 98, 100b, 111, 113, 120a, 124, 131, 135

Rodger McPhail: 42, 87, 97, 104, 108b, 109a

David Messum Ltd.: 72b, 116

The National Gallery: 23, 58b, 58c, 150

The National Trust: 63a

Clive Nicholls: 143

Kenneth Scowen: 10, 22a, 46, 129, 133, 138, 142b, 151

Spink & Sons Ltd.: 72à, 74

John Tarlton: 114b, 122, 127a–d, 142a

The Tate Gallery: 11, 37, 49

The Tryon Gallery Ltd.: 75c, 102, 103, 115a, 137, 139, 146

The Walker Art Gallery: 145

The Yale Center for British Art: frontispiece, 6a, 19, 34, 38, 50, 53, 63b, 68

The Game Conservancy at Fordingbridge.
Roger McPhail.

Index

Aelfric, Abbot   125
Aelian   124
Aeschylus   41
Alken, Henry Snr.   *31*, 66
Alken, Sam   *41, 70, 87, 135*
Alresford   *127*
Altcar   83
Amey Roadstone Corporation   139, *140*
Amusement   132
Anatomy of the Horse   65
Andrews, Mr and Mrs Robert   *58*, 61
Anderson, Douglas   *146*
Angler's Co-operative Association   130
angling   39, *72*, 124–127, *124, 126, 127, 128*
angling in sporting art   67, 68
Anne, Queen   79
Ansdell, Richard   *38*, 66, 68, *145*
Ascot Heath   79
Ashburton, Lord   112, 132
Ashdown Park   *37*
Atkinson, William   *58*

Bacon, Francis   15, 26
Badminton   *12*, 87
'bagging' foxes   93
Baker, D. J.   106
Barenger, James   *36, 101*
Barker, Thomas   *113*
Barlow, Francis   *63*, 64
Barnes, Juliana   125
Barret, George   *26*, 66
Batsby, John   *115*
battues   *111*, 132
Beaufort, 5th Duke of   87
Becher, Captain   83
Becket, Thomas   29, 44
Beckford, Peter   89
'Beiram'   *67*
Belvoir Hunt   *91, 95*, 132
Betjeman, Sir John   136
Bifrons Park   *7*
The Big Shots   111
Billesdon Coplow   96, 97
Birdsdall Clump   *91*
Black-neck *see* pheasant
Blaine, Delabere   28, 29
Blenheim Palace   13
Bletchingley   *142*
Blome, Richard   36, 39, 77, 88
Blubberhouse   116
Bohemia, shooting in   132, 134

Boke of St Albans   30, 125
A Book of Fishing with Hooke and Line   126
Botany Bay   96
Branscombe, G.   *109*
breckland, drainage of   118
Bretland, Thomas   *114*
'Brilliant'   *65*
Bristow, Edmund   *72*
British Birds   *72*, 99
British Field Sports   66
British school of sporting art   61
The British Shotgun 1850–1870   106
British Sporting Art Trust   71
British Sporting Paintings 1650–1850   70
British Zoology   45
Bryant, Sir Arthur   55
Buckenham   132
Buffon   42
bustard, great   118, *118*

Cannon Hall   116
capercaillie   146, *146*
Carnarvon, Lord   112
carp   125, *126*
Carta de Foresta   23, 29
Casson, Lionel   42
Charles II   79
Charborough Hounds   *91*
Cheltenham   *72, 82, 83*
chemicals in agriculture   137
Chequers Inn, St Albans   81
chub   *127*
Civil War, effect on game   85
Clandon Park   *63*
Clatworthy reservoir   *122*
Cobbett, William   94
Coke, Thomas (Lord Leicester)   57
Colchis   41, 42
Coleman, Edward   *72*
Coleman, Tommy   81
Colloquy of Aelfric   125
Colquoun, William   114
The Complete Gentleman   59, 94
Constable, John   *19*, 61, 68, *150, 151*
Cooper, Abraham   66, 68, *108*
country house, English   55
Country Landowners Association   149
The Compleat Angler   127, 128
Cordrey, John   *101*
coursing   *see* deer coursing, hare coursing
covert making   97, 109, 110, 135, 136

'Craftsman'   *35*
Cresswell Crags   *63*
Crichel   112
Cromwell   30, 36
crossbow   33
Crudgington, I. M.   106
crusades, influence of   24
Cudnam Hills   *101*
Curzon, Nathaniel   *65*
'Czarina'   87

Dalby, J.   *92*
Daniel, William   *119*
Daniel, Rev. W. B.   124
Darley Arabian   79
Davis, Charles   *26*
Davis, R. B.   *91*
Dean, Forest of   48
Dedham Vale   *19*
deer coursing   *12*, 28
deer hunting   23–28, *60, 62*
Deer and Their Management   15
deer parks   *12, 13, 14*, 13–15, *26*
Devis, Arthur   61
dogs
  development and breeding   37, 38, 87–89,
    112
  greyhound   *22, 36, 37, 37, 38, 56, 66, 67, 87*
  Labrador and Newfoundland   *66, 68, 72*,
    113, *114*
  pointer and setter   *7, 56, 58, 72, 98, 99*, 100,
    101, 115, 135
  spaniel   *41, 72, 109*
driving
  of grouse   116
  of partridges   *102, 103*, 104, 105
  of pheasants   106–110
duck   117–123, *117, 123*
Duleep Singh, Maharajah   112
Duncan, Edward   *117*
Duncton Hill   10

Earle, George   *116*
Earlom, Richard   68
Eaton Hall   *62*
Edge, Thomas   *18, 58*
Edward III   24, 29
Edward VII   *111*
Edwards, Lionel   69
Eley cartridge   101
Elizabeth I   29, 35, 37

Elmer, Stephen 68, *72*
Elvedon 112
Ely Abbey 125
enclosures *17*, 51, 52, *52*, *94*
Enclosure Act 50
Encyclopaedia of Rural Sport 28, 29
Erle-Drax, J. S. W. S. *91*
Essex Hunt *52*
Eusebius 94
Euston 112
Evelyn, John 48, 149
Evendon, Fred P. 144
Exeter, Lord *67*

Fairbrother, Nan 148, *148*, 149
falconry 29–32, *29, 30, 31, 32, 33, 43*, 77
farming 49–57, *49, 50, 53*
    open field system 49
    in 19th century 53
    in 20th century 57, *142, 148*
    crop rotation system 98, *98*, 131
    and game management 136, 137, *138*, 147–
      149
'Ferdinando' 80
Ferneley, C. L. *83*
Ferneley, John *18, 58*, 66, *66, 91, 95*
Fernie, Mr 97
ferreting *38*
fishing *see* angling
flight pools 121
Fordingbridge *140, 141*
forest and woodland
    clearance *17*, 47
    planting and regeneration 11, 48, 54, 109,
      110, 135, 136, 147–149
Forsyth's percussion system 101
foxhounds, breeding 88, 89
fox-hunting 35, *70, 71, 76*, 85, 88–97, *89, 91,
      92, 93, 94, 95, 96*, 99
A Frenchman's England 59
French partridge *99*, 104

Gainsborough, Thomas *58*, 61
The Game Birds and Wild Fowl of the British Isles 69
Game Laws
    early 24, 29
    of 1671 39, 93, 94
Gamonia, or the Art of Preserving Game 15, 132
garganey *139*
Garrard, George 66, 77
The Gentleman's Recreation *33*, 36, 39, 43, 77,
      77, 99, 152, 154
Gilpin, Sawrey 61, 66
Gladstone, Hugh 132
Golden Fleece, legend of 42
The Golden Peaches of Samarkand 41
Goodwood, *67*
goose *119, 121*
goshawk 31
Grafton, Duke of *89*
grain prices in 19th century 53, 54
Grand National 83
Granville, Lord *26*
gravel pits 138–144, *140, 141*
Graves, Robert 42

Great Exhibition of 1851 54, 105
Great Linford 139, *140*
Great Witchingham 112
The Greek Myths 42
Greener, W. W. 102
Greville, Mr *67*
greyhound *see* dogs
Grimston Park *113*
Grosvenor Hunt *62*, 65
grouse, red 114–116, *115, 116*, 144, 145, *145*
grouse, ruffed 146
Grouse Disease 115
Grunstone *91*
guns
    development of 33–35
    muzzle-loading *34*, 100
    breech-loading 105, *115, 145*
The Gun and its Development 102

Hachisuka 45
Handley Cross 97
Haldon Hall *11*
Hales, Sir Edward *34*
Hall Barn 112
Hall, General 105
Hanbury Hall 106
'Old Hardstaff' *18*
hare 84–87, *85*
hare coursing *36*, 37, *37, 38*, 56, *67, 83, 84, 87*
hare hunting *62*, 84–87, *87*
Harold, King 44
Harrison, Dr Jeffery 138
Harrison, J. C. *102, 103*, 137
Hatfield Forest 28
Hatfield House 132
Hawker, Col. Peter 101, 102, 113, *119*
hawking *see* falconry
Hayman, Francis 61
heather 114, *114*, 145
hedgerows and hedge planting 17, *17*, 48, *49,
      51, 52, 52*, 88, 97, 105, 131, 148, *148*, 149
Henley-on-Thames *17*
Henry III 26
Henry V 85
Henry VIII 36, 45
Henry, Prince of Wales 25
Herring, J. F. *53*, 66, *76, 94, 96, 115*
Hertford, Marquis of 104
Hertfordshire Hunt *93*
Heveningham Hall 105
Holkham Hall 57, 110, 132
Home, Lord 19
'Honest John' *62*
Hopkins, Gerard Manley 136
horse racing 35, 36, 60, *65*, 67, 69, *78, 80, 81,
      82, 83*
Hoskins, W. G. 12
hounds, development of 87–89
Howitt, Samuel 66, *78, 87, 120, 123*
St Hubert *23*, 24
Hunger's Prevention 33
hunting *see* deer hunting, fox-hunting, hare
      hunting
hunting, Continental attitudes to 35, 87
hunting livery, introduction of 94

Ibbetson, J. C. 66, *68, 134*
Institute of Terrestrial Ecology 145
Itchen, River *127*, 128

James I 29, 36, 84
Jansson, J. *14*
Japanese Green Pheasant 45
'Jason' *65*
Jason and the Argonauts 42
Jockey Club 80
John, King 24, 29
Jones, Willaim *40, 124*
Jorrocks 97
Joy, T. M. *131*

Kent, Mr *67*
King's Somborne 26
Kip *12, 13*
Kozicky, Ed 146
Kublai Khan 117

land ownership
    in Middle Ages 50
    in 19th century 54, 55
    modern 149
Labrador retriever *see* dogs
Landseer, Sir Edwin 68
Lang, Joseph 105
Laporte, G. H. *26*
Laxton 50
Leadenhall Market 93
Leicester, 1st Earl of 57
Leicester, 2nd Earl of 111, 112
Leonardo da Vinci 65
Leopold, Professor Aldo 146
Linford, Great 139
Linkenholt *47*
Liverpool Grand National 83
Lynn, Mr 83

Macdonald, G. F. 115
Malmesbury, Lord 113
Manton, Joseph 101, 102, 107
Markham, Gervase 33
Markham Arabian 36
marling 57
Marlow, William 66
Marshall, Ben 66
Marshall, William 52
Mascalle, Leonard 126
The Master of Game 85
McPhail, Rodger
Meggernie *145*
Mellon Foundation 71
Melton Constable *12*
Melton Hunt *59*
Melton Mowbray *18, 58*, 89
Mercier, Philippe *34*
Meynell, Mr 80
Meynell, Hugo 88, 89, 94, 96
Milan gun production 102
Milk Hill *22*
Millais, John 69
Monahan, Hugh 70, *72, 139*

Mongolian pheasant 45
Munnings, Sir Alfred 69, *72*
Mytton, Jack 94

Nacton 81
Napoleonic Wars 53, 94, 102, 104
National Hunt Committee 83
Natural History 42
Netherthorpe, Lord 17
Newfoundland *see* dogs
New Lives, New Landscapes 148
Newmarket 36, *65*, 79, *80*
Nimrod's Hunting Tours 97
Notting Hill Hippodrome 80
Nutscale reservoir *142*

'Old Rowley' 79
Orford 104
Orford, Lord 87
Osbaldeston, George 94

Palladius 44
Parker, Eric 45
partridge, common *78*, 97–106, *98, 99, 101,*
  102, 103, 137
partridge, French *99*, 104
Payne-Gallwey, Sir Ralph 18, 112, 132, 134
Peacham, Henry, 59, 94
Peake, Robert *25*
Pennant, Thomas 45
Pepys, Samuel 102
peregrine falcon 30
phasianidae see pheasant
Phasis, River 41
pheasant *38*, 39–45, *40, 41, 42, 43, 44*, 57, 106–
  112, *107, 109*
  black-neck *38*, 42
  Japanese Green 45
  Mongolian 45
  Reeves 41, 45
  ring-neck *38, 42, 44*, 45, *109*
pheasant, history of
  in China 40, 41
  in Golden Fleece legend 42
  in Roman world 44, *44*, 45
  in Western Europe 41
  in Britain, 44, 106, 108–110
pheasant rearing 132
Phillips, F. A. *111*
Phillips, Henry *150*
pike *124, 126*
Pisanello, A. *23*
Pollard, James 66, *67*, 68, *81*, 83, *93*
pollution of rivers 128, 130
ponds and reservoirs 119–123, *122*, 130, *140,*
  141, 142
Portland, Duke of 114
ptarmigan 116
Pure Rivers Society 128
Pye, Henry James 132

quail *99*
Quorndon Hall 88

rabbit *38, 124*
railway, influence of
  on countryside 53
  on fox-hunting 96
  on shooting 104, 110, 111, *145*
Raby Hunt *71*
Ram's Head Covert *59*
Rawstorne, Lawrence 15, 132
Raynham Hall 98
Record Bags and Shooting Records 132
Reed, G. *101*
Reed, T. *101*
Reinagle, Philip 68, *72*
Rhine, River 130
Richmond Park 26, *26*
Ripon, 2nd Marquis of 112, *113*
Ripuarian Code 29
de la Rochefoucauld, François 59
Rolfe, A. F. *126*
'Rubini' *67*
Ruffer, J. G. 111
Rural Rides 94
Rural Sports 124

St Albans 81–3, *82*
St Albans, Boke of 30, 125
Sandringham 110
Sartorius, Francis *7*, 64, *65, 80*
Sartorius, John Nost *7, 56*, 66, *71*
Savernake Forest 26
Schafer, Edward 41
Sefton, Earl of *145*
Seymour, James *37, 62*, 64, *84*, 87, *89*
Shafton, Mr 80
shooting *7*, 33, 34, *34*, 38, *38, 39*, 40, 41, 56,
  77, 97–116, *98, 101, 106, 107, 108, 109, 111,*
  113, 114, 115, 117, 119, 120, 123, 131, 134, 135
shooting parties 112, *113*
Six Mile Bottom 112
Smythe, Thomas *92*
snipe *120*
sparrow-hawk 31
Spode, A. *67*
Sport and the Horse 70
The Sportsman's Dictionary 13, 33, 37, 107
Sporting Art – England 1700–1900 60
Sporting Magazine 108
'Spry' 80
Squires, T. *101*
stalking horse 33, *33*, 100
Stantonbury Lake *140*
Steeplechasing 81–3, *81, 82, 83*
Stonehenge 67
Stonor, Sir Harry 112
Stubbs, George *frontispiece, 50, 62, 63, 63*, 64,
  65, *68*
Sudbury *58*
Surtees, J. 97
The Sunday Times 128
Swaffham Coursing Society 87
Sykes, Sir Tatton *91*

Tennant, John *26*
Test, River *127*, 128
Thacker's rules for coursing 37

Thames, River 130
Thames Trout and other Fishes 130
Thorburn, Archibald *72, 99*
Thornton, Col. Thomas 77, 101, 114
Thorpe Trussels 96
Throop *127*
timber use
  in Middle Ages 47
  in 18th century 48
Titus Andronicus 26
Towne, Francis *11*
Townshend, Lord 57, 98, 131
Trevelyan, G. M. 52, 53
trout *127, 142*
Turf Hotel, St Albans 81
Turner, F. C. *32*, 83
Turner, J. M. W. 68

Uffington White Horse 21
Utrecht, Treaty of 94

Vernon papers 106
Victoria, Queen 54

walking-up, introduction of 110
Walpole, Sir Robert 60, 89
Walton, Izaac 127
Walsingham, Lord 18, 112, 116
Ward, James *38*, 61, 66
Waterloo Cup 83
Watson, Dr Adam 145
The Way the Wind Blows 19
Wellington, 1st Duke of 54
West Dean 112
Weston Colville 105
'Whale' *67*
Wheeler, Alwyne 130
Whitehead, Kenneth 15
white horses 21, *22*
Whymper, Charles
wildfowl and wildfowling 22, *22*, 33, 117–123,
  117, 119, 120, 121, 123, 139
wildfowl management 139–144
The Wildfowler 22
Wildfowlers Association 138
wildlife management 144–149
Wildlife Society 144
Wilson, Richard 65
Wilson, W. B. *66*
Winchester *127*
Windsor Castle *26*
Windsor Great Park *26, 26*, 28, *60*, 79, 104
Woburn *49*
Wolstenholme, Dean *52*, 66, *85, 98, 107*
Woodchester *44*
woodcock *106, 107*, 108, *108*, 109
Woodland Harriers *92*
Woodstock 13
Woollett, S. 65, *68*
Wootton, John *7, 17, 30, 35, 60*, 61, 64

Yale Center for British Art 71
York, 2nd Duke of 85
Young, Arthur 98